HEROES OF HISTORY

ABRAHAM LINCOLN

A New Birth of Freedom

HEROES OF HISTORY

ABRAHAM LINCOLN

A New Birth of Freedom

JANET & GEOFF BENGE

Emerald Books

P.O. BOX 635, LYNNWOOD, WA 98046

Emerald Books are distributed through YWAM Publishing. For a full list of titles, including other great biographies, visit our website at www.ywampublishing.com

Abraham Lincoln: A New Birth of Freedom

Published by Emerald Books
P.O. Box 635
Lynnwood, Washington 98046

Third printing 2011

Library of Congress Cataloging-in-Publication Data
Benge, Janet, 1958–
    Abraham Lincoln: a new birth of freedom / by Janet and Geoff Benge
        p. cm. — (Heroes of history)
Includes bibliographical references (p.).
Summary: A narrative biography of our sixteenth president, focusing on his impact on history and the qualities of his character.
    ISBN 1-883002-79-6 (alk. paper)
    ISBN 978-1-883002-79-4 (alk. paper)
    1. Lincoln, Abraham, 1809-1865—Juvenile literature.
2. Presidents—United States—Biography—Juvenile literature.
[1. Lincoln, Abraham, 1809–1865. 2. Presidents.] I. Benge, Geoff, 1954– II. Title.
    E457.905 .B46 2001
    973.7'092—dc21   2001002815

ISBN-13: 978-1-883002-79-4; ISBN-10: 1-883002-79-6

Printed in the United States of America

HEROES OF HISTORY
Biographies

Abraham Lincoln
Alan Shepard
Benjamin Franklin
Christopher Columbus
Clara Barton
Davy Crockett
Daniel Boone
Douglas MacArthur
George Washington
George Washington Carver
Harriet Tubman
John Adams
John Smith
Laura Ingalls Wilder
Meriwether Lewis
Orville Wright
Ronald Reagan
Theodore Roosevelt
Thomas Edison
William Penn

More Heroes of History coming soon!
Unit study curriculum guides are available
for select biographies.

Available at your local bookstore or
through Emerald Books
1 (800) 922-2143

Contents

Free Passage

Captain Abraham (Abe) Lincoln looked up from cleaning his rifle. Were the men louder than normal? He gave the gun a final stroke with the oilcloth, stood up, and strolled over to the tents to investigate.

"The only good Indian is a dead Indian," Abe heard someone yell. He quickened his pace, every sense on high alert. As he rounded a tent, he saw a group of men from his company and from Major Stillman's company clustered in a circle. With his height he could see over their heads to the middle of the group, where an old Indian man stood clutching a piece of paper.

"It's a letter from General Cass," Abe heard the Indian say, his eyes wide with fear.

"A letter!" laughed one of the soldiers. "How's a letter going to protect you?"

"Let's get him!" yelled another man.

Just then Abe elbowed his way to the front. He took the letter from the old Indian and quickly read it. "This man is right. He has a letter allowing him to be in the area. He means us no harm," he told the group.

A shout of rage went up from the soldiers. "I enlisted to kill Indians, and here's an Indian. He's not getting out of here alive."

The hair on the back of Abe's neck stood up. Abe knew he had only a second to decide what to do. The men wanted to see blood spilled. Abe couldn't just turn and walk away and let the soldiers vent their rage on the old Indian man. Instead he pushed the old man behind him. "Whoever wants to harm him will have to kill me first," he vowed, looking the men under his command in the eye.

Abe saw rage in their faces, then resignation. He seized the moment. "Go on back to what you were doing," he ordered. "I'll take care of our visitor."

Slowly the men drifted away, and Abe escorted the Indian safely out of the camp and watched as he disappeared into the woods.

As he walked back to camp, Abe worried about the men. They were spoiling for a fight, and he knew from his own boyhood that when someone wants a fight, he usually finds one. He decided to keep his company extra busy with chores until they were on the move again.

Back at camp Abe sat down by the fire and poured some coffee from the pot simmering there into his tin mug. As he sipped the strong black liquid, he thought about the incident. Yes, the man with the letter was an Indian, and he and his men had been drafted into the militia to fight Indians, in particular Black Hawk and his men. But the letter from General Cass the old Indian carried conferred on him the right of safe passage, and Abe had to obey it. The United States was a country of laws. To give in and allow his men to take out their frustrations on the old man simply because he was the first Indian they had encountered on their campaign would have struck a blow at the very laws that bound the country together. If freedom of movement had been conferred on the Indian, then it needed to be protected at all cost. After all, the future of the country depended on the rule of law. People couldn't be allowed to do as they pleased, even out here on the frontier, where life was tough and surviving from year to year consumed the waking hours of most people.

Although he didn't know it then, this belief would serve Abe well as president of the United States, leading a divided country through its most difficult crises. But right then, sitting by the fire on the western frontier of Indiana, all of that was in the future, far beyond the imagination of the young man who as a small boy had come to the wilds of Indiana from Kentucky with his family.

Dispossessed

Seven-year-old Abraham Lincoln, or Abe, as everyone called him, stood peering out the door of the family cabin, scanning the road that passed by about a hundred yards away. The road was part of the Cumberland Trail, the main route from Louisville, Kentucky, to Nashville, Tennessee, and someone was always traveling on it. In the past ten minutes Abe had seen a gang of gaunt black slaves shuffling along, with a slave trader on horseback at the rear, whip in hand. A shiny buggy had also gone by. Abe's mother told him that the men who rode in such buggies were important people like congressmen and senators on their way to Louisville.

These days, though, what Abe liked to watch most were the covered wagons pulled by teams of

horses or oxen. Abe would catch a glimpse of someone his own age on one of the wagons and try to
imagine the excitement of heading into the wilderness. He hoped he would experience that excitement for himself soon. There was a possibility that
his mother, Nancy, his father, Tom, and nine-year-
old sister, Sarah, could be making their way along
the same road in December. This was not certain
yet, but seven days earlier, his father had ridden
off to Indiana to see if he could locate a suitable
plot of land for the family to settle on. Not that
there was anything wrong with the farm they lived
on in Hardin County, Kentucky. Abe liked the place.
But there was a problem—a problem Abe knew
about only because he had lain awake in his loft
bed late one night and heard his father talking to a
neighbor about it.

His ears had pricked up as he heard his father's
tone of voice; it was tired and defeated. Abe's
father, Tom Lincoln, hardly ever sounded like that.
He always had a funny story to tell or a song to
sing, but not that night. The two men had talked in
low voices about the problem of land ownership in
Kentucky. Abe didn't understand all they said, but
he was able to follow parts of the conversation. And
even to a young boy the situation seemed unfair.

Tom Lincoln owned three farms in Kentucky,
none of them large, but each of them big enough to
make a living from. But now lawyers were saying
he didn't actually own the farms. It was all because
of a law stating that when a person bought land in
Kentucky he had to survey it himself and determine

where the boundaries were. The law caused problems from the start. Some people simply lied about the boundaries of their property when they had their title deeds prepared, saying they had paid for land they knew belonged to their neighbors. Others made an honest effort to record where their land started and finished.

The trouble was that people used landmarks like trees, streambeds, piles of rocks, even clumps of dirt to mark out their land. But over time, these markers could change. A tree would topple, or a flood would force a streambed to flow in a different path. To make matters worse, most landowners in Kentucky, like Abe's father, could not read or write. To draw up the title deed for their land, they hired a clerk. Unfortunately, these clerks worked fast and often made careless mistakes, which an illiterate farmer had no way of detecting.

As a result of these problems, oftentimes three or four men had title to the same piece of land. As Abe continued listening from the loft, he learned that the Middletons, a wealthy family from Philadelphia, were taking advantage of the confusing situation. The Middletons claimed they had a title to the Lincoln farm at Knob Creek, as well as the nine other farms neighboring it. This totaled ten thousand acres of land, and the Middletons were determined to take the land from its current owners. They hired important lawyers from back east to make sure they got what they wanted. Hardworking, illiterate men like Tom Lincoln and his neighbors were no match for such an onslaught of fancy lawyers. They had no money to hire lawyers to defend their right of ownership and so were about to lose the land they had paid for with hard-earned money. It was then that Abe had first heard his father talk about heading north into Indiana Territory.

As bitter as his father sounded, Abe knew of one reason why his parents would be glad to leave Kentucky. When Kentucky had been admitted to the Union in 1792, it was declared a slave state. Slaves did most of the hard labor in the area, and during the past ten years, more and more slaves had been brought in to work the land. Now, in 1816, there were 1,627 white males over sixteen years of age and 1,007 black slaves living in Hardin County. Having so many slaves in the county made it difficult for uneducated white men to find work. Most of the farmers dispossessed of their land had no choice but to pack up and move on. Not only that, the Lincolns were members of Little Mount Church, a Separate Baptist congregation. There were many things members of the church did not believe in, such as drinking alcohol, cursing, smoking, gambling on horse races, and most important, owning slaves. It had been generally agreed that any new states west of the Ohio River would be free states, where there was no slavery, and Abe Lincoln's father was happy to contemplate living in a place where people were not owned like cattle.

As Abe had drifted off to sleep that night, safely tucked under his bearskin blanket, he hoped his father would find a new place for them all to live.

Now, a month later, Abe was standing in the doorway, craning his neck for a glimpse of his father's horse coming down the road. Abe's father had been gone a week now and was expected home any day. Finally Abe caught sight of the piebald stallion and saw his father waving at him. Tom Lincoln had a huge grin on his face, and Abe knew that could mean only one thing—they were moving!

"Hello, boy," Abe's father yelled as soon as he was within earshot. "Tell your mother to put the kettle on. I have plenty to tell you all."

Abe ran inside to tell his mother the good news. Soon the family was sitting around the stove as Mr. Lincoln sipped steaming hot coffee and told them about his trip. "I found just the right place for us," he explained, running a hand through his thick black hair. "It's a great spot, a quarter section in Perry County."

"Does it have a spring on it?" Abe asked, mindful that he would be the one carrying the water to the house. He didn't want to make the same long trek to a distant creek each day that some of his friends made to draw water.

His father chuckled. "There's a spring right about where we're going to build our cabin, and a stream on the northwest boundary, too. It's virgin woods, and there's plenty of wild game. The forest is filled with antelope, wildcats, raccoons, opossums, bears, and wolves. One thing is for sure: As long as I have powder in my rifle, we won't starve to death."

Abe was glad to hear that, though he had heard some hair-raising tales about wildcats and bears.

Tom Lincoln talked on, excitement ringing in his voice. "I went ahead and marked the boundaries with piles of brush and set up a camp there so others will know I have a claim on the land. But I think we should get there as soon as we can."

"Are you sure we can own it outright, with a proper title and everything in order?" Abe's mother asked, looking up from the sock she was darning as they talked.

"Positive! All one hundred and sixty acres of it," her husband replied. "President Madison issued a proclamation putting the land up for sale at two dollars an acre. The government has already surveyed the land, and it offers a guaranteed title on every piece. If all goes well, we'll have the $320 purchase price paid off in five years, and the land will be completely ours."

"Well, if we aim to be there by Christmas, we had better start packing," Mrs. Lincoln replied.

During the following days the family was engulfed in a swirl of activity. There was so much to be done. Corn had to be stored at the neighbors'. Tom Lincoln would come back for it once his family was settled in the new location. Neither of Abe's parents could see any point in taking furniture with them. There was limited room on the wagon for furniture once the food and farm equipment had been loaded. And besides, Tom Lincoln was one of the best carpenters in the county. He would have no difficulty making new furniture from the oak and hickory trees that grew on the new property.

Mrs. Lincoln examined every single item before it was loaded onto the wagon to make sure it was strictly necessary. The feather mattress and blankets made it on board, as did the spinning wheel, cooking pots and utensils, axes, plow tips, and Mr. Lincoln's tools. Tom would need them not only to make new furniture when they reached Indiana but also to build things and sell them to other pioneers to make some money while he and Abe got the new farm up and running.

When it was too dark to work any longer, the family gathered around the light of a single bear-grease candle. Mrs. Lincoln spun wool into yarn, Sarah patched clothes, and Abe and his father whittled pegs to hold together the large trunk they were taking with them. Abe loved this time together. His father always had an interesting tale to tell.

"Tell us about the old Indian who got murdered near our new property. You promised you would," begged Abe a few nights before they left for Indiana.

"Now, Tom," interrupted Abe's mother, "there's no need scaring the children. That's not a tale for little ones. They don't need to be up at night worrying about such things. And besides, there are no Indians left around where we're going to settle. You told me that yourself."

Tom Lincoln looked down at the floor sheepishly and changed the subject. "I took forty bushels of corn over to Jacob Robb's today. There's no way it will fit on the wagon. I'll come back for it in the spring. We hauled it up into the rafters in the barn. It should be safe there through the winter."

Abe went back to whittling, knowing his father would tell him the story another day, out of his mother's hearing. He decided his mother was worried about upsetting them with such a story because both he and Sarah were named after relatives who had gotten into serious trouble with Indians. Abe had heard the stories a hundred times from his father, and he thought about them as he whittled. Abe's grandfather, Abraham Lincoln, was born in Pennsylvania but had moved out into the wilderness of Kentucky. He had been a friend of the now famous Daniel Boone. One day when Abe's grandfather was out in the field sowing seed with his three sons, Mordecai, Josiah, and Tom, Abe's father, they heard the sudden popping sound of gunfire. Abe's grandfather dropped to the ground. The two older boys had been warned to be on the lookout for an Indian attack, and they sprang into action. Fourteen-year-old Mordecai ran for the cabin while Josiah sprinted off toward the neighbors for help. That left Abe's father, then six years old, frozen in terror, watching the blood drain from his father's body onto the freshly plowed earth. Life was never the same for Tom Lincoln after his father's death. Although the family never lacked for food, Tom had to help support the family as soon as he was able. By the time he was twelve, he was making his living as a farmhand.

As dramatic as Abe's father's story was, the story of the woman Abe's sister was named after was even more amazing. Sarah Mitchell was Abe's mother's cousin. She was six years old when she and her parents and older brother set out as part of a wagon train headed for Kentucky. They were nearing a place called Defeated Camp, just outside Crab Orchard Fort, when they heard whoops and war cries. A party of Indians, tomahawks in hand, descended on the wagon train. In the commotion that followed, it was every family for themselves. Sarah's mother was one of the first in the group to be struck by a tomahawk. Sarah's father grabbed a spear from an Indian who had been shot to protect his wounded wife until help arrived from the nearby fort. The two children were left to fend for themselves, and Sarah's older brother grabbed Sarah by the hand and pulled her away from the scene, hoping to escape into the woods. As they fled, three Indians crashed through the under-brush after them. The terrified children came to a stream. Sarah's brother scrambled over a log bridge and reached back for his sister's hand to help her across. However, fear rooted Sarah to the spot— she could not move. Within a second, two strong brown arms grabbed her from behind and lifted her off the ground. She was carried back to a wait-ing horse.

As Sarah was thrown up onto the horse, the scene she was leaving behind burned into her mind. Her mother lay dying beside the wagon while her father wrestled with an Indian. Sarah was sure she herself would not live to see the sunset, but she was wrong. The Potawatomi Indians who captured her kept her as a worker. Sarah traveled with them past the Great Lakes all the way into Canada. Five long years went by before she was released as part of a treaty agreement called Wayne's Treaty. Of course, Sarah immediately went in search of her family, only to find that her mother had died from her injuries and her father, who had survived the raid, had gone to look for her and had drowned in a swollen river along the way.

Sarah's Aunt Rachel, Abe's grandmother, took Sarah in. Sarah and her cousin Nancy, Abe's mother, grew up together, and many years later Abe's older sister was named after his mother's cousin.

"And don't let me forget to dig up the last few sweet potatoes in the patch behind the barn," Abe heard his mother say as he refocused his attention on the conversation going on around him. He rubbed his hands, which were cramping from holding the knife for so long. As he rubbed them, he wondered what adventures awaited him and his family beyond the safe confines of their farm at Knob Hill.

Chapter 3

A New Home

Giddap," Abe's father yelled as he flicked the reins. Eagerly the four horses took up the slack in their harnesses, and the wagon jerked forward. Abe checked to make sure the cow was tied securely to the back of the wagon and then turned for one last look at the only home he could remember. He had actually been born ten miles southwest of Knob Hill farm, where Nolin Creek forked, just outside of Hogdenville. But the Lincolns had moved when he was only two years old, and he had no recollection of his first home.

Several of the neighbors who had helped lift and arrange the sacks of grain, farm implements, and tools in the wagon stood outside the cabin and waved good-bye. The tallest of this group was Dennis, Abe's sixteen-year-old cousin. Whenever his mother allowed him to roam farther afield than around the cabin, Abe would walk to Dennis's cabin and trail his cousin around. He would miss Dennis most of all. Although he had little schooling, Dennis was a never-ending source of funny stories and practical jokes.

Abe wondered what would happen to the farm now that they were leaving. He supposed a neighbor would move into the cabin until the Middletons evicted them and combined the farms into a large plantation that would be worked by slaves.

Sweeping his eyes over the landscape, Abe paused to stare at the hilltop south of the cabin. He and his mother had visited the spot often to pray at the grave of Abe's little brother Thomas, who had died at three years of age. Abe wondered whether the new owner of the farm would honor the spot marked by a stone with the initials T. L. carved into it or cast the stone marker aside and plow the land.

"Come on, son, let's go," Abe heard his mother's voice break into his thoughts.

Abe linked arms with her and started walking. The wagon was not large enough for all four of them to ride at once, so Sarah had chosen to take the first turn sitting up front beside her father while Abe and his mother walked behind.

It was midmorning when they set out, and Mr. Lincoln hoped to travel twenty miles by evening. The entire trip was about a hundred miles, but he warned the family that the last sixteen miles— through rugged woods with no trail—would probably take longer than the rest of the trip combined.

Soon they passed the tiny schoolhouse where Abe and Sarah had attended class for several months. Abe smiled as he recalled his days there. He had been sent to school more to keep Sarah company than to learn himself. But as it turned out, he was the one thirsty for knowledge. Within a month of arriving at school, he could read and was starting to write the letters of the alphabet. Paper was scarce, so Abe wrote on anything he could find. He used a stick on freshly fallen snow, a knifepoint in the soot on the bottom of a pot, even a nugget of charcoal on an old piece of firewood.

Abe's family puzzled over where his intense interest in learning came from. After all, his father could not read or write, and although his mother could read, she had never learned to write a word. She simply wrote an X as her signature. And Sarah plodded along with reading, which seemed such a chore to her.

Abe smiled to himself as he walked. He might be leaving school behind, which was open only when a teacher was passing through the area, but he was not leaving learning behind. In the trunk at the back of the wagon he had the means to teach himself. Tucked inside the trunk was a copy of the Dilworth spelling book, the only book besides the Bible the Lincoln family owned. It was a class textbook, and Abe knew it was much more than a book on how to spell words. It had chapters on American general knowledge, roman numerals, and best of all, poems and fables. As he walked along, Abe set himself a goal. During the long winter nights in

Indiana, he was going to learn every single thing in the book.

After walking for about three miles, Abe's feet began to drag. "How far to the Ohio River, Ma?" he asked.

Mrs. Lincoln smiled down at him. "It's a long ways off yet, son, but what a sight it will be!" she said.

Abe tried to imagine a big river like the Ohio. His father had told him all about it, but somehow he couldn't picture it. The only two bodies of water he had ever seen were the creek that ran through the farm and the local spring. He knew the creek flowed into the Salt River, which in turn flowed into the Ohio River. But that gave him no picture of what the Ohio was like. His father told him that paddle steamers, huge flat-bottomed boats with a big wheel on the back that churned the water, sailed up and down the river. Abe had never seen anything that was not powered by a person or animals. The idea of something using steam to make it go fascinated and puzzled him, all the more so since paddle steamers plied a river he had never experienced and could not imagine.

Along the way they passed individual cabins and small settlements of three or four cabins clustered together. As they went by them, Abe was not surprised at the friendly tones they were greeted with. His father had a knack of becoming friends with most people he met. He always had a pair of willing hands to offer to someone in need.

As soon as the sun began to set, a chill seeped up from the damp ground and engulfed them. It was time to find a quiet spot to spend the night. The family laid out animal hides on the dirt beside the wagon and nestled together beneath a bearskin and a feather quilt. Even with all his clothes on and his mother hugging him close, Abe shivered most of the night. He was more than ready to help his mother make a fire and cook hot cornmeal mush the next morning. Then they were on their way again.

On the third day, Abe was sitting up on the wagon when he recalled the story his mother had stopped his father from telling him several nights before. "Tell me the story about the old Indian now," he urged his father.

Tom Lincoln looked down at his son. "I don't know. It could be the type of story that would scare a young one like you," he replied, though the smile in his eyes told Abe his father was about to do the thing he did best—tell a story.

"It was five years ago, back in 1811, and a small distance from where our new cabin is going to be, that an old Indian named Setteedown lived with his wife, a few sons and daughters, and a man by the name of Big Bones."

Abe nodded, taking in everything his father said.

"Well, Setteedown lived with many memories. He remembered when the land belonged to his tribe, the Shawnees, and they hunted and fished there. Most of the Indians had been moved on by then, but not Setteedown. He wanted to stay put."

Mr. Lincoln flicked the reins before continuing. "One day, Setteedown must have got to thinking about all the things the white man had taken away from him, and he decided to take revenge on some-one. A family by the name of Meeks lived closest to where he set his traps along the Little Pigeon Creek. One summer's day, Setteedown, along with one of his sons and Big Bones, ambushed Atha Meeks as he came down to draw water from the creek. Settee-down shot the boy in the knee. Atha's father heard the shot and came running. The old Indian set his sights on him and shot Mr. Meeks dead. And then the three of them set upon Atha with tomahawks.

"Soon Atha's Uncle William came running to see what the commotion was. He shot and killed Big Bones, and Setteedown and his son fled into the woods. A posse of neighbors was formed to hunt them down. There was no jail anywhere around, of course, so when Setteedown was caught he was placed under arrest in a justice of the peace's cabin. The posse was supposed to guard him, but during the night Setteedown was shot to death. Had to be the uncle, everyone said, but no one asked any questions. The following week the posse cleared out the last few Indians in the Little Pigeon Creek area, and now there isn't a single one to be seen."

Abe sat quietly for a while, rubbing his cold hands together and thinking about what his father had told him. Although the threat from Indians no longer existed where they were going, they had plenty of other dangers to worry about, everything from bears to wildcats.

Finally, on the fourth morning, the family reached the crest of a hill. "I see it. I see it. Abe, come quick!" Sarah yelled.

Abe ran to the front of the wagon and swung himself up beside his sister. He gasped. Far to the north, framed between two huge oak trees, was a wide swath of water the color of a rain cloud.

"Yep, that's the Ohio River. Grand, isn't it?" Mr. Lincoln said.

Abe nodded. Images from the many Bible stories his mother had read to him sprang to mind. There was Noah and the great flood that covered the earth. And Moses parting the Red Sea to escape from the Egyptians. And Jesus preaching from a boat on the Sea of Galilee. Abe could imagine them all so much better now that he had seen the Ohio River.

More wagons and people on foot joined the Lincolns as they approached Thompson's Landing. A barrel-chested man with the longest mustache Abe had ever seen waved at them as their wagon rolled toward the small wooden jetty on the river-bank. Abe felt his mother's hand clamp down on his shoulder. "Don't get ahead now, son," she said.

When Abe looked up at his mother, he could see fear in her eyes at the prospect of crossing the river. Abe didn't share her fear. To him the Ohio River was the most wonderful sight he had ever seen. It glistened like silver ribbon in the midday sun. And as they got closer, he saw several wide barges loaded with barrels and sacks of grain floating downstream. "Where are they going, Pa?" he asked.

"New Orleans, most likely," his father replied.

Soon the Lincolns' wagon rolled onto the barge that ferried people, horses, and wagons across the Ohio River. Chunks of wood were jammed under the wagon wheels so that the wagon would not roll, and the horses and the cow were tied up firmly. Mr. Lincoln pulled some coins from his money pouch and counted out one dollar, twelve and a half cents, the fare for carrying the wagon, horses, cow, and family members across the river.

Mr. Thompson, the barge owner, gave the order to cast off. Two men, one on either side of the barge, began pulling on long poles that reached to the bottom of the river. Mr. Thompson guided the barge from the back with a long, wide-bladed steering oar. The current in midstream was fast, and icy cold water splashed up at Abe, who hardly noticed. He was too intent on taking in every part of the adventure.

"Pity there's no paddle steamers today," Mr. Thompson remarked. "Earlier this month the *Washington* and the *Pike* came down the river on their way to New Orleans. Amazing to see those huge paddles thrashing the water."

"How far is it to New Orleans?" Abe asked Mr. Thompson.

"It's over a thousand miles, and none of them without dangers," came the reply.

Abe tried to take in the information, though he had no idea how far a thousand miles really was, other than it was a long, long way.

Mrs. Lincoln smiled with relief when the ferry reached the other side of the river without incident. The family came ashore in Indiana just above where the Anderson River runs into the Ohio. It was December 11, 1816, an important day for the

Lincoln family but more so for Indiana. It was the day Indiana Territory officially entered the Union, becoming the nineteenth state in the United States of America.

Only one trail led away from the river, and the Lincolns followed it as they set out on the next stage of their journey. The trail ran north for twelve miles to Polk Patch, but the Lincolns would turn off before then and set out into the wilderness toward their new property.

In a few places the trail was wide and clear, but most of the way it could be identified only as a narrow opening between trees. It was also covered with fresh snow. And the farther they walked, the colder Abe felt. His new long buckskin breeches worn over his old pair and the two linen shirts his mother had made in the fall could not keep him warm. His coonskin cap did keep his ears warm, but it had been a long time since he'd had any feeling in his nose. At night the family did their best to stay warm, huddled together around a campfire. By the second day on the trail, Abe's sense of adventure was wearing thin. He began to wonder if they would ever make it to their destination.

The snow turned to slush, and thick fog descended, giving the surrounding dense forest an eerie quality. Abe tried not to think about the animals that roamed among the trees, though every twig that crackled made his heart skip a beat.

Finally, early on the third day, they reached the spot where Mr. Lincoln announced they would have to leave the trail and strike out on their own.

This was a sobering moment for Abe, who had been studying the forest along the way, with its thick, vine-tangled undergrowth. Abe hoped by some miracle that when they reached the turnoff, the land would be clear and grassy, but it looked more impenetrable than ever.

"Six miles to the north lies our new home!" Mr. Lincoln said, jumping down from the wagon. As he pulled two axes from the back and handed one to seven-year-old Abe, he said, "Come on. It's time to do some men's work."

Abe hacked at the vines and bushes while his father cut down the larger trees. Sarah scrambled along behind Abe, throwing the cut vines and bushes aside. Mrs. Lincoln was firmly in charge of the wagon now. She urged the horses forward over the unfamiliar, roughly cleared ground. By the end of the day they were all exhausted. Abe's hands were a mass of blisters, and he was glad to lay his weary body down on a pile of underbrush.

"This here's the corner of our farm," Tom Lincoln proudly announced to his family after they had been hacking their way through the wilderness for three days. "It's only a little farther to the place where I set up the campsite."

His words seemed to spur everyone on, and they kept pushing forward until they came to a rough clearing with a small shack in the middle of it. "There's the shack I erected," Mr. Lincoln declared.

Abe decided that "shack" was too grand a description of the place. It had three walls of sticks lashed together and a roof of dry brush. It offered less shelter than sleeping huddled up beside the wagon. Silence fell over the group as they looked around at their new home.

"We'll start building a cabin first thing in the morning. Right now let's put some brush down on the dirt floor so we don't have to sleep in the mud," Mr. Lincoln said.

With his blistered hands, Abe picked up the axe and walked over to the nearest stand of brush, overwhelmed at the task that lay in front of them all.

Chapter 4

Little Pigeon Creek

With a lot of coaxing, Tom Lincoln was able to get a fire going, and the family huddled together around it through the long night. As dawn broke the next morning, Abe's father woke him. It was time to start unloading the supplies from the wagon.

"How long will it take to build a cabin, Pa?" Abe asked, adjusting the suspenders that held up his trousers.

"If we put some muscle into it, shouldn't take more than a week," his father replied.

Abe heaved a sigh of relief. The thought of spending more time sleeping out in the open scared him. He had sat up half the night listening to the various screams and squawks coming from the forest. Even the long periods of silence had somehow seemed frightening to him.

"I reckon we'll build the cabin right over there," continued his father, pointing to the edge of the clearing. "There's a bit of a rise, which will keep the damp from settling on the floor. And we'll get a good view once we've cut down the trees."

Abe looked around at the enormous trees that surrounded the clearing. He knew they would all have to be cut down and the ground prepared in time for spring planting.

Mrs. Lincoln stirred and rubbed her arms against her body. "Good morning," she said, shivering. "Sarah and I will feed the fire and make some mush."

"I'll head over to Little Pigeon," Tom Lincoln said, pulling a bridle over his piebald stallion's head. "I hope to come back with some help. Abe, you can start grubbing out the area where the cabin is going to be built. Keep your eye out for some good corner stones."

As Abe watched his father disappear into the woods on horseback, he cheered himself up with the thought that neighbors would soon be arriving to help. Helping one another was the pioneer way. The first thing a smart man did when he made a land claim was to introduce himself to his neighbors. When a cabin needed to be built, everyone pitched in, knowing that in turn, neighbors would help them in time of need.

By the time the winter sun was high in the clear sky, Abe's father had returned with six men from nearby farms. One of them handed Mrs. Lincoln a clay jar of honey. Mrs. Lincoln thanked the man and set about making a pot of coffee.

It was too cold to stand around, so the men went straight to work. Abe could see that they had built cabins before. They worked hard, with little talking. Four of the men chopped down oak and hickory trees while the other two stripped away the branches. Then, using the horses, Mr. Lincoln dragged the logs into a pile.

While the men worked, Abe grubbed away at the ground where the floor of the new cabin would be. The dirt was partially frozen, and it took a lot of energy to break up the ground and smooth the lumps into a floor.

Abe had seen cabins being built before back in Kentucky, and he knew that they needed about forty logs around a foot in diameter. Abe's father measured the logs with his feet. Those for the back and front walls of the cabin needed to be twenty feet long, while the logs for the sides were two feet shorter.

By the following evening, all the logs had been cut down and assembled into a pile. It was time to begin building. With great excitement, the men rolled four round stones up from the creek and laid them at the corners of the new cabin. Next, they laid two logs in place, one to begin the front wall and the other the back wall. Notches were cut in the ends so that two more logs could be fitted into them to form the base of the side walls. Abe watched as the process was repeated and the walls began to take shape.

"You can start on the chinking," Abe's father said, pointing to Abe and Sarah. "The ground is too frozen, and so we won't be able to make daub until it thaws. But, Abe, you can split some smaller pieces of wood, and Sarah can stuff them into the bigger holes between the logs."

The children set about the long job of stopping the holes while the men continued to put up the walls. By the next afternoon it was time to put up the roof joists and the ridgepole. All that remained was to make clapboards for the roof, make a chimney to go up the outside of the cabin, and cut holes for the doorway and the fireplace.

Abe thought about the grease-paper window in their old cabin. He knew his father would not be making holes for windows in the new cabin, at least not yet. Nor would he be making beds. Every ounce of energy he and the family had would need to go into clearing the land so they could plant crops in spring.

Within ten days of arriving at their land claim on Little Pigeon Creek, the Lincolns had moved into their new cabin. Everything had to be kept off the damp dirt floor until the fire had time to dry out the interior. Abe didn't mind. He was glad to have a door that swung closed on leather hinges. When it was shut at night, he felt safe from the animals that prowled outside. The cow, which was allowed to roam freely during the day looking for food, was tethered to the west wall of the cabin at night. Abe's father slept on the other side of that wall, ready to leap up and rescue the cow at the first sign of a disturbance.

Once the cabin had been built, life for the family quickly fell into a monotonous routine. Abe and his father went out at dawn to cut down small trees and bushes, which they piled up around the larger trees. Sarah and Mrs. Lincoln labored hard to keep the fire burning. It was all they had to keep them warm and to cook food and heat water. And when they had used up their supply of candles, it was their only source of light at night. Since the "men" of the family were busy clearing land, Mrs. Lincoln had to keep the family supplied with fresh game. This was not hard, because huge flocks of carrier pigeons flew overhead and there was a constant scurry of smaller critters, such as squirrels, groundhogs, and weasels, in the forest.

Occasionally the sky would glow orange, and Abe knew that someone nearby was burning off his land. Indeed, soon it was time for him and his father to do the same. Between them they had cleared the brush and small trees from about five acres of land and stacked them around the trunks of the larger trees. Now it was time to set the piles on fire.

Soon the sky above the Lincolns' land glowed orange too. Great billows of smoke blocked out the sun, and Abe felt the heat against his cheeks as he watched flames engulf tree after tree. Animals and birds scattered in all directions, and Mrs. Lincoln watched anxiously, hoping that a falling cinder wouldn't set the cabin roof on fire.

The fire burned for three days. When it was over, five acres of once wooded land had been reduced to a blackened, smoldering field with an occasional smoking tree stump sticking up in it.

Now it was time to clear away these stumps and haul off the rocks so the land would be ready to plow in the spring.

Everyone in the Little Pigeon Creek area was too busy breaking in land to pay social calls, and Abe had no idea whether there were other boys his own age around. He wished he had someone else to talk to besides his parents and Sarah. But since he didn't, each evening after dinner he would lose himself in the Dilworth spelling book, memorizing Roman numerals and reading and rereading the poems and fables until he could recite them by heart.

About the only group activity that punctuated the grind of life was a bear hunt. Bears were the most feared animals in the forest. They were powerful and fast and the enemy of every farmer. They trampled crops and killed pigs, sheep, and cows. Sometimes they even went after a person. When a bear got too close to a cabin site, the local men banded together for a bear hunt to kill the troublesome animal.

On February 10, 1817, just two days before Abe's eighth birthday, a community bear hunt was announced, and Tom Lincoln went off to join in. Abe, though, was too young to go along, and so he sat on the doorstep whittling a new stirring spoon for his mother. He worked away intently. When he looked up, a group of wild turkeys was no more than a few feet away, busily pecking at the newly cleared ground. Silently Abe backed into the cabin and shut the door. "Ma, can I use Pa's spare gun?"

he asked. "There are turkeys near the door, and I think I can shoot one."

His mother looked at him for a second. Abe knew she was weighing the value of the gunpowder against the chances of his hitting something edible. He had never shot anything before.

"All right," she agreed. "But you only get one shot, so you'd better make it count."

Abe took his father's spare flintlock rifle, loaded it with gunpowder and lead shot, and prepared to shoot. He peered through a gap between the logs. The turkeys were still there. His heart pounded as he poked the barrel of the gun through the gap and aimed it at the closest turkey, a large male that strutted about proudly, its feathers spread wide. Abe's finger closed on the trigger.

Bang! Blood spurted from the breast of the turkey as it collapsed to the ground, while the recoil of the gun caused Abe to fall backward.

"Well done!" Mrs. Lincoln exclaimed as she swung open the door to see what he had shot. "You'll make a great hunter one day."

Abe stepped outside and walked over to the fallen bird. As he looked at its lifeless body, his stomach began to churn. He had killed this magnificent creature, and he felt terrible about it. He knew without a shadow of a doubt that he would never hunt or kill another animal as long as he lived.

Later that night, as they sat around the fire eating the boiled legs of the turkey, Abe's mother recounted the story of its demise. She made Abe sound like a hero as he sat quietly, choking down the meat.

Finally the snow began to thaw, swelling the creek with swiftly moving water and bringing new life to the trees. Nature was coming alive again after its winter rest. It was time to plant the corn. First the freshly thawed ground had to be plowed. This proved to be a backbreaking task. Abe and his father worked together from sunup to sundown, plowing the charred earth. Abe's job was to walk beside the plow, pulling stones and pieces of gnarled root out of the way, while his father plodded along behind the horse, guiding the plow. Once in a while Abe found an Indian arrowhead. He collected these and kept them in a leather pouch beside the fireplace.

Mrs. Lincoln and Sarah were hard at work, too. Now that spring had come, it was time to wash their clothes and blankets. And the thawed dirt could now be mixed with grass to make daub to fill the gaps between the logs in the cabin walls. For the first time since leaving Kentucky, Abe went to sleep without a bitter draft on him.

Once the land was plowed and the weather was warm enough, the first crop of corn was planted. It was a tense time as the family waited to see whether a late frost would kill off the tiny shoots that pushed their way up through the soil. Thankfully, spring was mild and the corn grew high and strong. However, this was not a time for a pioneer family to rest. Wooden rail fences had to be erected to protect the crops, and Abe's father kept clearing more land in the hope that he could plant a later crop as well.

By fall everything was running smoothly. The first harvest was not huge, but it was enough to get them through the winter and provide enough seed corn for the following spring. They were all in high spirits, being able to eat something besides wild birds and small animals. In addition, the forest beyond the clearing was filled with wonderful things to eat. There were huge wild blackberries, crabapples, cherries, and plums, as well as acorns and other nuts. Once in a while Mr. Lincoln even took the time to follow buzzing bees to a hive. Then, once the tree had been cut down and the bees smoked out, the family had delicious sweet honey to put on their corncakes.

The Lincoln family felt relieved that they had survived the wilderness and the winter. They now had a windproof cabin, cultivated land, and a store of dried food. Mr. Lincoln decided that it would be possible in a year or two to make a good living from the farm. Before the first snow of the approaching winter arrived, he set out for Vincennes to pay a deposit on the land.

Two neighbors, Bill Whitman and Noah Gordon, rode with him. The three of them all entered their deposits at the county courthouse on October 15, 1817. Abe's father claimed 160 acres of land, for which he was paying two dollars an acre. He paid only sixteen dollars that day, but the clerk assured him it was enough to secure title to the land. When he got back, Tom Lincoln told his family how happy he was to pay the money over to the government for a guaranteed title. Unlike in Kentucky, this time there would be no lawyers to cheat him out of the land.

The second year at Little Pigeon Creek passed much the same as the first. There were more trees to burn, more land to plow, and more crops to plant and harvest.

About three times a year a circuit-riding preacher would come to Little Pigeon, and the Lincolns would ride over to hear him preach. This, along with the monthly trip to the local mill to grind corn, was the only time Abe saw other boys, and he made the most of every minute with them. He loved to listen as they told stories of life on the frontier. He even had a few stories of his own to add.

One afternoon on his way back from chopping firewood, Abe stopped to watch a flock of bright green Carolina parakeets. Their green and yellow bodies swooped and glided on the gentle breeze. As Abe watched, he heard a noise. What was it? He cocked his head to listen. It was someone yelling. It was a male voice but not his father's. He broke into a run and headed for the cabin. As he burst into the clearing, he let out a whoop of joy. A wagon was standing in front of the cabin, and beside it were his Aunt Betsy and Uncle Tom Sparrow. And best of all, Dennis, Abe's cousin, was with them. The two of them ran to greet each other.

"You're getting pretty big now, Abe," his cousin remarked, roughing up Abe's dark hair. "Now don't you forget I was the second person to ever hold you when you were a baby. I took one look at you and said you'll never amount to much."

Abe laughed loudly. He had heard his cousin tell the story many times before, but it never sounded as good as it did this time.

Mrs. Lincoln ushered everyone into the cabin to enjoy a pot of coffee. As the older family members began to talk, Abe learned that the Sparrows' farm in Kentucky had suffered the same fate as theirs. Too many people thought they owned parts of the farm. Finally Uncle Tom had packed up and headed out to join the Lincolns at Little Pigeon Creek.

"We'll get on our feet as soon as we can," Aunt Betsy apologized. "We don't mean to be a burden to you, and we have enough provisions to last through to summer."

Abe's father stood up. "You only have to look around to see that there's not enough room in here for three more bodies. How about you make your- selves at home in the old shack, and we'll find you a good piece of land and get a cabin up for you before it snows."

There was a murmur of agreement inside the cabin. As soon as they had finished their coffee, they all went out to help the family unload their belongings into the old shack. Abe wove some twigs and brush between the stick walls to plug up some holes. As he worked, he kept glancing over at Dennis. He could hardly believe it. His favorite rel- ative was going to be living nearby. They would be able to fish together and swim on hot summer afternoons. He would show Dennis his stash of Indian arrowheads and tell him the story of Settee-down and Big Bones.

That night Abe drifted off to sleep happier than he had been in a long time. He had no way of knowing that a black shadow was about to fall over the two families now living in the clearing.

Chapter 5

Changes

"M a! Ma! Aunt Betsy's cow has the trembles," Abe yelled as soon as he was within shouting distance of the cabin.

His mother appeared at the door, stirring spoon in hand. "Are you sure? Did you ask Uncle Tom if that's what it was?" she replied.

Abe nodded, big tears welling in his eyes.

"God have mercy on us all," Mrs. Lincoln said, putting her arm around nine-year-old Abe. They stood in the autumn sunlight together, engrossed in their own thoughts. Abe could not remember the first time he heard about cow trembles and milk sickness. It was a shadow that hung ominously over every pioneering family. It started when a cow began to shake violently. The shaking did not stop until the cow dropped dead, usually in about three days. But that was not the worst of it. Before the cow showed any signs that it was coming down with the trembles, it gave poisonous milk—milk that killed anyone who drank it. No one knew how milk sickness started, but it was a dreaded name to every pioneer.

Abe finally found the courage to voice his worst fears. "But what about the quilting bee last week? You and me and Sarah, we were all in Aunt Betsy's cabin. We all ate and drank there."

Mrs. Lincoln nodded. "We can only wait and see what God brings," she replied.

The Lincoln family did not have to wait long. Within two days, the cow was dead and Uncle Tom was in bed with severe stomach cramps and an unusual thirst, both sure signs of milk sickness. The nearest doctor was thirty miles away, but there was no point in calling him. There was no cure for milk sickness. Once a person came down with it, he was doomed. Mr. Lincoln began making a coffin.

Abe watched as Uncle Tom made out his final will, which his mother and Aunt Betsy witnessed and signed. Uncle Tom died the next day. That same afternoon, Aunt Betsy went to bed with the same symptoms. She also died quickly, and Tom Lincoln made a second roughhewn coffin. Abe and Dennis dug the graves, and Tom and Betsy Sparrow were laid to rest near their cabin.

Later that night as the Lincolns and Dennis sat gloomily around the fire, Mrs. Lincoln dropped the shirt she was darning.

"Is everything all right?" Abe asked.

"Yes, I'm just feeling a little dizzy from today," she said.

Four pairs of eyes looked anxiously at her. Dizziness was not a good sign.

By the following morning, Nancy Lincoln was obviously not well. She insisted on getting up, but everyone could see she was in great pain. She carried on as best she could for three more days, until finally she admitted defeat and went to bed to die. The family tiptoed around her, trying to think of some way to save her life, but they all knew there was nothing they could do.

From her bed Nancy Lincoln called Sarah and Abe to her side. She looked as white as the pillow she was resting on as she reached out to hold their hands. With supreme effort she opened her eyes and looked at her children one last time. She spoke to Abe. "I am going away from you, Abraham, and I shall not return. I know that you will be a good boy and that you will be kind to Sarah and to your father. I want you to live as I taught you and to love your heavenly Father."

She started to speak to Sarah, but Abe could not stay by her bed a moment longer. He sat down on the stool by the fire and wept.

Later that day, October 5, 1818, thirty-four-year-old Nancy Lincoln died. Abe's father and Dennis whipsawed a log into planks. As the two of them planed the planks smooth, Abe whittled pegs from pinewood to hold the coffin together. No one said a word. There was nothing to say. The three of them dug a grave for Nancy next to the Sparrows.

By lunchtime the next day Mrs. Lincoln was laid in the coffin on the kitchen table. One by one the neighbors, including Peter Brooner, who had lost his wife to milk sickness only days before and was left with eight young children to raise, came to pay their last respects.

It was a clear, crisp day and the oak and maple trees were a blaze of orange and red when Nancy Lincoln's coffin was carried from the cabin to the gravesite. Young Lamar, an elder in the church in Little Pigeon, spoke briefly as Mrs. Lincoln was buried. With her was buried the last of Abe's happy childhood. Something changed in him that day. From then on he was always aware of how easily life could be snatched away.

After the funeral those in the Lincoln household went into shock and depression. Dennis moved into the cabin, but he was no replacement for a mother. February came and Sarah turned twelve and Abe ten, but there was no celebrating.

Sarah did what she could to cook, scrub clothes, tend the fire, and mend the clothes, but these were exhausting tasks for a twelve-year-old to do day in and day out. She missed her mother terribly, and when Abe came in from the fields, he often found her sitting by the dwindling fire, sobbing. Dennis brought her a turtle and a baby raccoon that he found in the woods, but they did little to console her.

Slowly the family fell into disarray. Abe and Sarah seldom bothered to wash themselves, and they were often hungry. There was no more rabbit pie or deer stew for dinner. Their clothes were worn, ripped, and dirty. No one wanted to go into Little Pigeon Creek to hear the circuit-riding preacher. They all just stayed at the farm and moped.

Finally, fourteen months after Nancy Lincoln's death, Abe's father made an announcement. "I'm going back to Kentucky to find another wife," he told his children.

The whole idea startled Abe. He had never thought of anyone, much less a stranger, replacing his mother. He wondered what this woman would be like. Would she like him? Would she make him wash in cold water every morning? Would she read the Bible to him every Sunday like his mother had? Would she be able to read at all?

Abe had only one way to answer his questions, and that was to wait until his father had returned. Abe and Dennis had plenty to do around the farm, but even so, Abe found time to agonize over the arrival of a stepmother.

It was just before Christmas 1819 when Abe heard the rumble of wagon wheels in the distance, followed by giggling and yelling. Abe peered out the door of the cabin to see his father sitting proudly on a wagon piled high with furniture. Beside him was a tall woman wearing a large white bonnet and a dark blue dress. Scampering alongside the wagon were three children. Abe stood speechless as the wagon rolled up beside the cabin. Never in his dreams had he thought of his father bringing back stepbrothers or stepsisters!

Abe's father swung down from the wagon in one powerful move. "Look lively, boy," he said. "This is your new ma and your three new kin, Elizabeth, Mathilda, and John."

Abe continued to stand there, aware that his pants were laughably too short on him and his shirt had a hole at the elbow. His hair hadn't been cut for so long it fell in his eyes. Abe smiled weakly. "Welcome," was all he could think to say. The girls, whom Abe judged to be about thirteen and nine, giggled, and Abe felt his ears turn red with embarrassment.

By now Mr. Lincoln had helped Abe's new stepmother down from the wagon, and she was making her way determinedly toward the cabin door. She stood and looked in for a moment, eyeing the dirty piles of bedding and Sarah sitting shyly beside the embers. "I can see what you mean about this place needing a woman's touch, Tom!" she laughed.

Something in her laugh made Abe relax. He could sense that his new stepmother was not laughing at them, and he silently thanked her for that.

By nightfall everything was unloaded from the wagon and wedged inside the cabin. There was barely room to walk between the chest of drawers, the table, the chairs, and the clothes press that the family had brought with them. There were also mounds of bedclothes and feather quilts. All of this luxury made Abe realize that his stepfamily had been used to a much higher standard than living in a one-room, dirt-floor cabin. He waited for the grumbling to begin, but it never did. Everyone seemed happy to be "home."

Over the next week or so Abe learned more about his new family. His stepmother's name before she married his father was Sarah Johnston, though everyone called her Sally. Her first husband had been the Hardin County jailer until he died of cholera three years before. Sally and Abe's father had known each other most of their lives, having grown up in the same area.

John, the youngest child in the family, was a year younger than Abe, though much shorter. He loved the idea of being a woodsman and trailed along behind Abe wherever he went. He chattered continuously, too, but Abe didn't mind. It had been a long time since he'd had a boy about his own age to talk to.

With one woman and three girls now working in the cabin, it was amazing how quickly the place was transformed into a clean and orderly home. Sally Lincoln asked Abe's father if he and Dennis could lay a wood floor in the cabin. Abe was surprised when his father not only agreed to the improvement but also began work on it the very next day. Once the floor was down, everything stayed much cleaner.

Sally then set her sights on the sleeping arrangements. "A loft," she said to Abe a week after her arrival. "A loft would make a lot more room. I'll ask your father if he can make one right away."

Once again Abe's father happily complied. Nicks were cut into the log walls to make a ladder, and a floor was put in the rafters. When the loft was finished, the three young males, Dennis, John, and

Abe, slept in it while Abe's father and stepmother slept in a new pole bed in one corner of the cabin. In the other corner, Mr. Lincoln made another pole bed for Sarah, Elizabeth, and Mathilda to sleep in.

Eight people from three different families were now living in a single cabin eighteen by twenty feet. It could have been a very trying arrangement, but everyone showed a great deal of tolerance. At night when it was time for bed, all of the males stood and stared at the fire while the females changed into their nightgowns. Then Mrs. Lincoln and the girls came and stood by the fire while the males changed. They reversed the procedure in the morning.

Abe watched carefully to see if his stepmother would treat her own children better than she treated him and Sarah. She did not. She treated everyone equally. Abe loved her for that, and it was not long before he found himself singing as he worked and looking forward to Sally's wonderful meals.

There was something else Abe liked about his new stepmother. She had brought four books with her: *Webster's Speller, Robinson Crusoe, Lessons in Elocution,* and *Arabian Nights.* Abe sat up night after night, reading until the fire's embers had grown too dim for him to see. He then got up at first light to continue reading. Everything about the books thrilled him. He loved the way they smelled, the way the pages flipped over, and their smooth leather covers. And the stories they contained fueled his imagination throughout the day. With a shovel in his hand, Abe was transformed from just a plain farm boy digging a garden to a pirate burying stolen treasure or a castaway looking for a fresh water supply.

The arrival of Sally and her three children changed Abe's life for the better. Within weeks his stepmother had even sewn him a new shirt and pants. This was just as well, because times were changing for the entire Little Pigeon Creek area. A new community known as Gentryville had sprung up around a newly established trading post, and it had become a hub of social activity. Most of the land around the Lincolns' farm had now been broken in. As a result the settlers finally had time to visit one another, and soon wagon ruts through the woods turned into rough roads as more wagons and carts traveled them. By the time Abe was twelve years old, many of the tasks the early settlers had done alone were now community events. There were regular corn-shucking days, hog killings, wool shearing, and quilting bees for the women. These events were exciting to Abe, but nothing was more exciting than the announcement that a Mr. Crawford had agreed to conduct a school session for two or three months.

Abe's father and stepmother encouraged Abe and Sarah and their stepsiblings to attend classes, even though it would cost two dollars each to send them. One week later, Abe was seated on a backless wooden bench.

"Ready, go!" Mr. Crawford announced, and the room erupted into a babble of noise as each student chanted or read aloud. Abe was used to this approach to teaching. Mr. Crawford ran a "blab school," much like the school Abe and Sarah had attended back in Kentucky. All the students were required to read or chant their lessons aloud at the same time so that the teacher could be sure they were all concentrating on their work. If a student stopped, a swift swat to the side of the head got the unlucky boy or girl back on track fast!

Sometimes the class sat quietly as Mr. Crawford lectured them on manners. On one of these occasions, Abe got bored and wrote a poem in the front of his math book. It read,

Abraham Lincoln is my name,
And with my pen I wrote the same.
I wrote in both haste and speed
And left it here for fools to read.

Every Friday they had a dreaded spelling test. Abe didn't fear it himself, as he was a good speller, but he felt sorry for some of the other students in the class who did not seem to have much natural ability when it came to spelling. One of these students was a girl named Ann Roby. One Friday Mr. Crawford barked out the word *defied* for her to spell aloud to the class.

Ann started out strong. "D-e-f..." Then she began to flounder. Abe guessed she was confused as to whether a "y" or an "i" should come next. He caught her attention and pointed his long finger at his own eye. Ann caught on to what he was doing. She gave a confident smile and finished spelling, "i-e-d."

Abe particularly enjoyed the opportunity to learn more math. He had found it easy to learn to read, but he needed a teacher to help him with long division and working out ratios. This was called "ciphering to the rule of three," and by the time school had finished, Abe probably knew more about it than anyone else in the area.

After three months Mr. Crawford announced that school was over for the year. He also told the students that he would not be coming back to teach again, and he did not know whether another teacher would be passing through anytime soon. This was a huge disappointment to Abe, but Mr. Crawford did one thing that helped soften the blow. He generously gave Abe two books—Parson Weems's *Life of George Washington* and an autobiography of Benjamin Franklin covering the first years of his life.

Abe had never read a biography before, and it opened his eyes to many things he had never considered. He read about Benjamin Franklin's experiment with electricity, a description of a library, and a trip to England. He also read about the Revolutionary War and the first President of the United States. The book about George Washington had woodcut pictures of famous battles of the war and maps showing where they were fought. This was all new information to Abe, who soaked it up like rain on parched earth.

Abe could not, however, spend all his time reading. When he turned thirteen, he was nearly as tall as his father, who was six feet tall, and his growth showed no sign of slowing down. Money was in short supply on the Lincoln farm, and now that Mr. Lincoln had John Johnston to help him with farm chores, he often hired Abe out to neighboring farmers. All the money Abe earned through this arrangement was paid to his father, since a boy was legally required to hand over any money he earned to his parents before he came of age at twenty-one.

Abe worked hard. He split rails for fences and plowed and hoed fields. Wherever he went, he carried one of his books with him, and in his spare moments he read a line or two and tried to memorize it. Using this method he rapidly learned chapter after chapter of his favorite books by heart. When he was not memorizing passages from his books, Abe thought about the life his father and Dennis lived. Dennis had married Abe's stepsister Elizabeth Johnston and settled on a nearby piece of land. Abe asked himself whether that was what he really wanted for his future. Somewhere deep inside of him he knew it was not.

Abe pondered over Benjamin Franklin's life. Franklin had come from a poor family like his. He had been the thirteenth of seventeen children. He had a haphazard education, and he loved to read. His autobiography showed how he had improved himself with hard work and self-discipline. Eventually he had served in the Continental Congress and helped to draft the Declaration of Independence. The fact that his story was true inspired Abe like nothing else he had ever read. Abe determined he would not spend his life toiling on a farm in the middle of nowhere. No, he would keep reading any and every book he could get his hands on, and one day, somehow, he would find a way out of farming.

Chapter 6

On the River

It was a hot summer morning in August 1826 when seventeen-year-old Abe Lincoln set out with Dennis and his friend Squire Hall to make some fast money. Their plan was simple. They would ride their horses down to the banks of the Ohio River and set up a wooding station for steamboats. A wooding station was a huge stockpile of neatly chopped wood that steamboat captains would buy to fuel their boats' boilers. Since Abe was one of the fastest men with an axe in the county, the trio figured they could make a lot of money supplying wood. They had been told a cord of wood would fetch as much as twenty-five cents, though sometimes a captain would pay for the wood with merchandise from his steamer rather than cash.

After a half-day ride, the three young men arrived at the riverbank, where they set up a lean-to to live in. Despite the fact that cutting the wood was hard work, Abe loved living on the river. The Ohio River was a main transportation route, and there was a steady stream of activity on the water. Paddle steamers carrying people and cargo rumbled their way upstream and downstream. And all manner of other craft, such as keelboats, flat bottom boats, rafts, scows, rowboats, and canoes, also plied the waters. And then there were the people who made their way along the riverbank on foot and horseback—circuit-riding preachers, traders, merchants, and pioneers.

Abe particularly enjoyed loading wood onboard the steamboats. As he did so, he would talk with the captain and engineers, who told him amazing tales of life on the river. Abe would retell these stories to the people at the general store in Troy, the small community close to where they had set up their wooding station.

Troy also had a post office, where Abe was introduced to a new source of reading material—newspapers. Papers were delivered regularly to the post office and were available free to anyone who could read them. Abe read these newspapers as often as he could. Soon he began keeping a scrapbook into which he copied the news items and editorials he found interesting. He even tried his hand at writing a few editorials himself.

By the end of summer, the three young men added up what they had earned. It was nowhere near as much as they had hoped to make. In fact, all Abe had to show for his backbreaking labor was nine yards of white cotton fabric, payment from one captain. It was time for the men to think seriously about their future as businessmen. Dennis and Squire Hall were both married and decided to return to the Little Pigeon Creek area and try to coax a living from their farms once again.

Abe, however, found it hard to imagine going back home, especially now that he had heard so many stories about life up and down the river. He agonized over what to do. Should he return to help his father and maybe marry and settle into farm life as his sister Sarah had done just over a year before? Or should he stay and try to find work on the river? Eventually he decided to stay on the river a little longer.

Abe presented himself to James Taylor, who operated the ferry that crisscrossed the Anderson River just upstream from where it flowed into the Ohio River. The crossing was one hundred feet wide and fifteen feet deep. Abe could see that Mr. Taylor was sizing him up, and he drew himself up to his full height of six feet four inches and puffed out his skinny chest. Mr. Taylor slapped him on the back. "You look like you're itching for a job, son," he laughed.

Soon a deal was struck. Abe would live with the Taylors, sharing a room with Green, their twelve-year-old son, and eating his meals with the family. In addition, he would be paid six dollars a month.

Abe came to enjoy his work on the ferry. And even though the job did not pay much, he had lots of opportunities each day to talk to people and learn new things. When there were not enough passengers to warrant taking the larger ferry across the river, Abe would row a small boat across. Word soon spread that if the water was low, Abe Lincoln could row from one side to the other with just one sweep of his strong, gangly arms.

It wasn't long before Abe decided to put his carpentry skills to work and build himself a boat. The boat led to a different kind of adventure from anything Abe had planned. One day two men in a wagon pulled up to the small landing. The wagon was promptly unloaded, and the older of the two men looked wildly around. He spotted Abe and rushed over to him. "Do you have a boat, young man?" he asked.

"Yes, sir," Abe replied, pointing to his newly built scow.

"The *General Pike* anchored there in midstream is due to leave any minute now, and my son and I have to be on board. Will you take us to it?"

Abe glanced at the paddle steamer in the middle of the river. They didn't have a minute to lose. Smoke billowed from its two stacks, and the second mate was preparing to pull up the anchor.

"I'll do it," Abe agreed, running back to the younger man and lifting a large carpetbag onto his shoulders. Within a minute the luggage was all on board and Abe was rowing frantically for the steamer. He was relieved when the captain spotted him. He knew almost everyone on the river by now, and he was sure the captain would wait for him. The captain did wait; the two men were soon clambering aboard the steamer, and their bags were then passed up.

As Abe turned back toward land, he heard two clinks in the bottom of the boat. He looked over his shoulder to see his two passengers peering down at him over the side of the paddle steamer. "Much obliged," yelled the older man.

When he had reached shore, Abe looked in the bottom of the boat. He found two shiny half-dollar coins, which he scooped up, hardly able to believe it. The men had paid him a dollar for twenty minutes' work! It seemed like a fortune to Abe, and it got him thinking.

The next time he saw someone arrive at the landing in a hurry to catch a paddle steamer, Abe stepped forward and offered to row them out to the boat. Soon he had a steady business going.

One day after he had taken a passenger to a steamer, Abe saw a man beckoning to him from the Kentucky side of the river. Abe wondered what the stranger wanted, so he rowed over to find out. As he got nearer, the man disappeared. His curiosity pricked, Abe pulled his boat ashore. As he did so, two men jumped out at him from behind a bush. They rushed at him, but then stopped short. Abe looked from one man to the other.

"You're that Abe Lincoln who takes passengers out to the steamboats, aren't you?" asked the man who had waved at Abe.

Abe nodded.

"Well, we were going to dunk you in the river, but on second thought, we should just talk."

"About what?" Abe asked.

"About you breaking the law, that's what. I'm Len Dill, and my brother John and I have the official license to ferry people across the Ohio River, and you owe us all the money you have made."

Abe stood quietly, thinking about what they had said. John Dill broke the silence. "You're not going to get away with it, you know. Samuel Pate is a justice of the peace, and he has a warrant out for your arrest."

"He does?" Abe asked, astonished.

"That's right, and we're all going to see him right now," Len Dill said.

Abe could see that he would have to resolve the problem, and so he went with the Dill brothers to see what was to be done. When the three men arrived at Samuel Pate's house, Mr. Pate read the law to them. "If any person whatsoever shall, for reward, set any person over any river or creek, whereupon public ferries are appointed, he or she so offending shall forfeit and pay five dollars for every such offense."

Abe gulped. Five dollars for each time he had carried a passenger to a boat! He would be paying this debt for the rest of his life. "May I see the law you just quoted?" he asked respectfully.

Mr. Pate handed the book to Abe, who quickly scanned it. His eyes stopped on one phrase, "set any person over any river or creek." It was the word over that caught his attention. "I have never ferried a passenger over the Ohio River," Abe said. "It is true that I have ferried them partway across from the Indiana shore, but I have always stopped midway and put them safely on board a boat."

Mr. Pate chuckled to himself. "You'd make a fine lawyer!" He turned to the Dill brothers. "Has young Mr. Lincoln ever dropped a passenger off on your side of the river?" he asked.

Both brothers shook their head.

"Then I have to agree with the defendant. Insomuch as he has not ferried anyone over the river, he has not broken any Kentucky law. The case is dismissed."

Abe turned to shake the Dill brothers' hands, but the men were already walking away. John Dill looked back with a scowl on his face.

"Do you have time for a drink?" Mr. Pate asked Abe. "Come and sit down and tell me all about yourself."

An hour passed quickly, and by the time Abe left, he had made a new friend and had an invitation to come back and visit Samuel Pate anytime he wanted. From then on, whenever Abe did not have any passengers, he would row over to the Kentucky side and listen as Mr. Pate heard the cases brought before him.

Before long Abe began thinking about how he would have argued for or against the issues in a case. Slowly but surely, he found himself fascinated by the law. Eventually, though, after another summer on the river, Abe decided to return home to help his father with the harvest. He was also eager to see Sarah and her husband, Aaron Grigsby, again, since his sister was pregnant with her first child.

Abe found life back in Little Pigeon Creek boring and uninspiring compared to life on the river. Still, his father kept him busy, first on the family farm and then working for neighbors. And when the first snow of winter fell, Abe was hired out to do carpentry work around the area.

On January 20, 1828, Abe was making some shelves for Sarah's father-in-law's smokehouse. He was planing a plank when Aaron Grigsby came running into the yard. Aaron was as white as a sheet. Abe stood up, his heart pounding as he wondered what the problem was.

"It's Sarah," Aaron gasped as soon as he got his breath. "She died just five minutes ago, and our baby girl was stillborn."

A strange numbness crept over Abe's body. He did not say a word. He sat down in the doorway to the smokehouse, placed his hands over his face, and sobbed. Sorrow washed over him in great waves. He could hardly bear to attend Sarah's funeral and watch her coffin lowered into the ground next to his mother's grave. Indeed, it was a long time before Abe smiled again, and an even longer time before he forgave Aaron Grigsby for not sending for the doctor soon enough when Sarah was about to give birth.

Before long Abe knew he had to leave Little Pigeon Creek. There were just too many sad memories, and the river was beckoning him again. Just as he was wondering what to do about it, James Gentry, after whom Gentryville was named, made Abe an offer he couldn't refuse. He needed a hired hand to help his nineteen-year-old son Allen take a cargo of corn and sweet potatoes downriver to sell in New Orleans. Abe could scarcely believe it. Not only would it get him away from Little Pigeon Creek and all the sad memories, but it finally gave him the chance to follow the paddle steamers downstream to the delta of the Mississippi River. He could hardly wait to get started on the journey.

Chapter 7

A Vast and Varied Country

Before they could head downriver to New Orleans, Abe and Allen Gentry had to build themselves a flat bottom boat. Beside the Ohio River at Rockport, where Allen lived, they amassed a pile of poplar and oak planks. Because of its straight and even grain, the poplar was used to build the hull of the boat, which was about sixty feet long and sixteen feet wide. When they finished the hull, it was rolled over and slid down the bank into the river. Then Abe and Allen used the oak planks to put a fore and aft deck on the boat, as well as a small cabin. From the oak they also fashioned long, wide oars and a rudder. One set of oars was placed at the front of the boat and another set at the back. Soon the craft was ready to be loaded with cargo.

In late fall, once the load of corn and sweet potatoes was securely stowed in the boat, the two young men set out on their journey. They rowed out into the middle of the river and headed south. The current on the Ohio River was slow, and they found themselves having to do more rowing than they would have liked. Abe worked the front oars while Allen worked the back and guided the boat with the rudder. At night they pulled over to the side of the river and slept.

It was not long before they left behind all the familiar places. As they rowed downstream, Abe closely studied the surrounding countryside. On both sides of the river, lush forest extended right to the water's edge. Dotted amid the forest were small communities much like Troy and Rockport.

After rounding a sweeping bend, Abe and Allen came to the place where the Tennessee River flowed into the Ohio. On the sandy flats where the two rivers joined, Abe spotted large flocks of wild turkeys. Three days later the two men reached the confluence of the Ohio and Mississippi Rivers. The first thing Abe noticed was that the current in the Mississippi was much swifter than the Ohio and he didn't have to row as much. He also noticed that there were now few communities dotted along the riverbank. They were making their way through large swaths of seemingly uncharted and unexplored land.

Although they saw few people on land, plenty of people were traveling in various boats on the river. Large paddle steamers trailing long streams of smoke from their stacks swished their way up and down the river. Passengers on these boats would wave and call out greetings as they went by. Abe and Allen were not the only ones taking a flat bottom boat downstream. As other rivers ran into the Mississippi, more boats joined the procession of vessels headed for New Orleans.

After a while, Abe began to notice that the countryside was changing. They were in the South now, and the large cypress trees that lined the river were festooned with Spanish moss.

Finally the town of Natchez, Mississippi, came into view. With a population of five thousand, it was the largest community Abe had ever seen. They tied up the boat at the edge of the river, and wide-eyed Abe strolled around the markets.

Before long it was time to head downstream again. They passed Baton Rouge, one hundred fifty miles from New Orleans. Below Baton Rouge were many large sugar plantations, protected from the surging water of the Mississippi by levees on both sides of the river.

One night Abe and Allen tied their boat up at the side of the river beside Madame Duchesne's plantation. For dinner they cooked several ears of corn from their cargo over a fire on the riverbank. They ate, and then exhausted, they climbed back onto the boat and went to sleep. Abe wasn't sure how long he had been asleep when he woke with a start. He listened for a moment. Had he heard a noise? Yes! Someone other than Allen was on the boat. Abe leapt out from under his blanket to see who it was. In the moonlight he saw seven slaves from the plantation trying to steal their cargo. He yelled to Allen and grabbed a length of wood from the front of the boat.

Abe stretched out his long arms and swung the piece of wood like a club. The wood thumped into two of the men, knocking them off balance, and the men fell overboard into the muddy water of the Mississippi River.

Before Abe could swing his club again, one of the other men lunged at him. As he fell to the deck, Abe dropped the wood and grabbed the man. Hand to hand they wrestled. At the same time, Allen attacked the men from behind with an oar. The robber yelled in pain as Abe twisted his arm behind his back. Soon a third slave was splashing in the cold water of the Mississippi.

Abe raced to help Allen, who was now under fierce attack. He swung his arms wildly as his fists pounded into the men. Finally the four remaining men fled the boat. Abe and Allen jumped off after them. They chased them into the woods and then ran back to the boat. Abe cut the mooring line, and he and Allen quickly paddled out onto the river before the would-be robbers could regroup and mount another attack.

When they felt safe, Abe and Allen examined each other's wounds. Abe had a cut above his right eye, and he tied a bandanna around his head to stem the flow of blood. The cut would leave a scar he'd have for the rest of his life.

Three days after the encounter with the robbers, Abe and Allen finally arrived in New Orleans and tied up their flat bottom boat alongside the many others moored there.

Abe, who had been awed by the size of Natchez, with its five thousand residents, could scarcely fathom a city like New Orleans, with a population of more than forty thousand. It had people from every race and color. British, French, Spanish, Mexican, Creole, Irish, and American people all shared the streets. And not only were there people from all over the world there but also the harbor was filled with ships waiting to load and carry goods around the globe. Abe read in the newspapers that there were ships ready to depart for such far-flung ports as Hamburg, Gibraltar, Aberdeen, Bremen, and Vera Cruz and American ports like New York, Providence, Philadelphia, and Baltimore.

After they had sold their cargo at the bustling market alongside the levee, Abe and Allen explored the narrow streets of New Orleans. The houses that lined the streets were two-storied, made of brick and mortar, and packed close together. Large windows swung open to the street to let in light and the cooling breezes that wafted in from the river. Upstairs, balconies adorned with ornate iron-work ran around the front of the buildings. Abe had never seen houses like these before. Almost every house he had seen to this point in his life had been made of logs.

As he walked the streets, Abe came face-to-face with something he hadn't seen since he was a small boy back in Kentucky—groups of slaves chained together being marched along. And worse, as he peered into the dark recesses of some of the buildings lining the streets, he realized they were slave markets. Black men, women, and children were being sold like cattle. Seeing human beings treated in such a way greatly disturbed Abe.

Finally, after several days of exploring New Orleans, it was time for Abe and Allen to head the 1,222 miles back upriver to Rockport. This time, though, they would not be taking the flat bottom boat. They sold the boat and bought tickets on a paddle steamer. Abe had been on paddle steamers before, loading wood, but this was the first time he had ever ridden on one. He stood on deck watching as the large pistons that turned the paddle wheel hissed to life. The wheel began to turn, and the boat moved upstream. Abe continued to stand on deck as they retraced the journey past Madame Duchesne's plantation. He felt the cut above his eye; it still hurt. He watched as Natchez disappeared behind them and the Spanish moss-covered trees of the South gave way to the type of woods he was used to seeing.

By the time he arrived back in Rockport, three months after setting out, Abe was amazed at just how vast and varied the United States really was.

Mr. Gentry paid Abe twenty-four dollars, eight dollars for each month he was away. With money in hand, Abe returned to the farm at Little Pigeon Creek. Since he was still not of legal age, he gave his earnings to his father and set to work around the farm.

The next year passed slowly for Abe. There was another outbreak of milk sickness that scared the whole community. Soon people began to talk about heading west into territory newly opened to settlers. The Lincoln family also began to discuss the idea among themselves. Eventually Abe's father and stepmother decided to sell their property and move on. Going along with them would be Abe and his three stepsiblings, their spouses, and their children—thirteen people in all.

Tom Lincoln managed to get $125 for the eighty acres of land he had purchased so far, the one hundred hogs he was raising, and five hundred bushels of corn. It was less than he had paid for the land, but it was the best he could do. When it was combined with some investments Sally Lincoln had made before her marriage to Abe's father, they had a total of $500 to take with them.

The group decided to head about one hundred twenty miles northwest to Macon County, Illinois. John Hanks, a relative of Abe's mother, had written to the family telling them how fertile the land was there. Abe did not have to accompany his parents, since he had come of age in February and no longer needed to seek his father's permission to do what he wanted. However, he was eager to help the family settle into their new home while he decided what he would do next. He wrote to John Hanks and told him they were on their way.

On March 1, 1830, three wagonloads of people and belongings set out from Little Pigeon Creek. Two of the wagons were pulled by oxen, and the third by horses. As they started, Abe thought about the journey the family had made to Little Pigeon Creek from Kentucky fourteen years before. It seemed like an eternity away to him. So much had changed in his life since that time.

The journey to Macon County was every bit as hard as the trip from Kentucky had been. The weather was beginning to warm, just enough to thaw the icy ground during the day and turn it to slush. Then it would get cold, and the ground would freeze solid again overnight. The rivers and streams were swollen with freshly thawed snow and were treacherous to cross.

At one stream, Abe's small dog lost its footing and fell in. Abe could not bear to lose the animal, so he leaped into the waist-deep, icy-cold water to rescue it. He grabbed the dog and placed it on the ice at the edge of the stream before clambering out himself. The dog seemed to bounce right back, but Abe shivered for the next two hours.

Once they had crossed the Wabash River, the seemingly endless prairie of Illinois replaced the forests of Indiana. Even on his trip to New Orleans, Abe had never seen anything quite like it before. Mile upon mile of long, waving grass stretched to the horizon. The settlers they passed on their way across the prairie had made huts for themselves from sod. They told the Lincoln family stories of how the roots of the grass were so strong that they had broken many metal plow tips trying to cultivate the land.

Everyone was glad when the little wagon train finally reached John Hanks's farm in Macon County. John had picked out a homesteading site for them. Since there were too many people for the group to stay with him, John guided them straight to the site he had picked out on the banks of the Sangamon River, just west of Decatur. Thankfully, there were trees in the area, and John had already chopped down and trimmed enough logs for them to build a single cabin. Abe, his father, John

Johnston, and Elizabeth's and Mathilda's husbands set to work. They did not want to spend one
more night out in the open than was absolutely
necessary.

As soon as the cabin was completed, they con-
structed a barn and a smokehouse and cleared fifteen acres of land just in time for planting. Once
again Abe was called upon to split rails for fences.
And once he had split enough for the new Lincoln
farm, he split three thousand rails for a neighbor.

In late spring they planted a crop of corn,
although the harvest was not as great as expected.
Tom Lincoln hoped it would be enough to get them
through winter to spring, when he would try to
coax a better crop from the soil.

One day during the summer, Abe got to make
his first political speech. He was in Decatur buying
provisions for his stepmother when he noticed a
crowd forming in the street. He strolled over to see
what was happening. It was a campaign meeting,
and two candidates for the state legislature were
debating the pros and cons of spending money to
improve the Sangamon River to make it more
accessible to large boats.

Abe listened with rapt attention. When the two
men were finished debating, one of them invited
anyone in the audience who had something to add
to the debate to speak up. Abe could not turn
down the opportunity. He stepped forward and told
the story of his recent trip down the Ohio and
Mississippi Rivers to New Orleans. He outlined all
the advantages of having a navigable, deep river
connecting the town with those farther downstream.

He told the crowd that he believed it was part of the government's role to help keep the rivers deep and uncluttered from debris and logs so they could be used efficiently to move people and freight. He then went on to praise Henry Clay's progressive agenda, which included improving transportation, adding protective tariffs, and creating a national bank. In finishing his speech, Abe painted a wonderfully bright future for Illinois, provided citizens were prepared to work together and support a government that would work for the common good. When he was done, people applauded enthusiastically.

As he walked home, Abe thought of ways he could have improved his speech and explained things better and how he could have worked more homespun stories into it. He promised himself he would be more prepared when the next such opportunity to speak came along. However, that would not be anytime soon. Winter was fast approaching, and some of the old-timers who gathered in front of the general store in town predicted it would be a hard one.

The old-timers were right. The Lincoln clan had never seen anything like it. In early December a blizzard blew through, dumping two and a half feet of snow on the ground. Temperatures fell below zero, and more snow fell. Soon the drifts were four feet deep. The cattle, hogs, and horses became easy prey for wolves as they stood helpless in the frozen wasteland. The adults ventured outside only when they absolutely had to. Still, one after the other, members of the group came down with chills and fevers. The temperature dipped to twelve degrees below zero and stayed there for days. None of them had anticipated such a prolonged period of cold, snowy weather, and soon there was not enough wood to keep the fire burning.

It was February before the weather began to warm slightly. Hardly an animal had survived the icy onslaught, and worse, several neighbors had frozen to death in their cabins. It was too much for the group. They never wanted to spend another winter like that, and so Mr. Lincoln decided to abandon the new farm and head a hundred miles southeast to Coles County. This time, though, Abe did not go with them. Now aged twenty-two, he wanted to strike out on his own and leave the backbreaking work of farming behind to earn his own money in his own way.

Chapter 8

New Salem

No one was surprised when Abraham Lincoln headed for the river again. Denton Offutt, a businessman with big plans, hired Abe to take a flat bottom boat loaded with barrels of pork, corn, and live hogs downriver to New Orleans. Denton Offutt promised Abe that if he did a good job he would hire him to run the new general store he was planning to open at New Salem, located along the Sangamon River. Abe recruited his stepbrother John Johnston and relative John Hanks to help him.

Abe was enthusiastic about his new opportunity, except for having to sew shut the eyes of the hogs so they would remain calm on the trip. He hated to see animals hurt in any way.

A little more than two years after his first visit, Abe arrived back in New Orleans. After the cargo and boat had been sold, he once again spent time taking in the sights of the city, with its varied architecture and culture. After a week relaxing in New Orleans, it was time to board a paddle steamer for the trip upriver to Illinois.

All went well on the return journey, and in Springfield Abe handed Denton Offutt the money he had received for the boat and its cargo. From Springfield Abe made his way by raft downriver to New Salem, where he arrived on July 31, 1831.

The following day Abraham Lincoln voted for the first time. The election was for local officials, and Abe stepped forward to declare his choice. He spoke in a loud, clear voice as the clerk of elections placed a mark on the tally sheet beside the candidate he gave his vote to. Since most people on the frontier could not read or write, they called out who it was they were voting for and a clerk wrote it down.

It took Abe until the end of September to build a log store and get all the supplies needed to stock it. Abe built a small room at the back of the store, where he slept. Business started off briskly. New Salem was a growing town of about twenty-five families set on a bluff above the river. Along with the new general store, the town had a barrel maker, a cobbler, a blacksmith, a hatter, a wheelwright, two doctors, and two saloons. It also had a courthouse, presided over by a justice of the peace named Bowling Green.

Abe had never lived in a community quite this large before. Many interesting people came into the store, and Abe made friends with them all. One man, Jack Kelso, at first glance seemed to be an uneducated drifter who lived in a shack and hunted and fished for his food. However, Abe soon discovered that Jack Kelso loved plays written by William Shakespeare and poems by Scotsman Robert Burns. Kelso could recite passages an hour long from memory, and he offered to loan Abe some of his books. Soon the two of them were reciting passages back and forth to each other.

Another educated man in New Salem was Dr. John Allen, who had come west to improve his health. He started the New Salem Debating Society in his living room, and Abe was a founding member. Schoolteacher Mentor Graham also attended the society meetings, and he and Abe quickly became friends. Mentor Graham loaned Abe grammar and mathematics books, which Abe studied during quiet times at the store.

When business was slack or there was a particularly interesting case being heard at the courthouse, Abe would close the store and go and listen to Bowling Green settle cases. Green noticed Abe's interest and began asking Abe to make a few comments on a case before he decided it. Abe did such a good job of summing up the core of a case in a logical way that people began asking him to represent them before the court. Although Abe could not do this officially because he did not have a license to practice law, Bowling Green gave him a book of legal forms. With this book Abe was able to help people draft documents such as wills and deeds. He got a great deal of satisfaction from helping farmers in this manner.

All in all, Abe was pleased with his new life in New Salem. He had proved to himself that he could make a living—fifteen dollars a month—without farming or splitting rails. As well, he had many new friends to talk to and learn new things from.

Denton Offutt told everyone he met that Abe was his best employee. In his opinion, Abraham Lincoln was smart, honest, funny, and as strong as an ox, by far the strongest man in the area. This last piece of information reached the ears of the Clary's Grove boys, a group of aimless young men who hung out at a saloon on the west side of New Salem. The leader of the group, Jack Armstrong, considered himself the strongest man for miles around, and he was not happy that the claim was being made about someone else.

One day after Abe had been in New Salem about three months, the Clary's Grove boys rode into town. Abe watched as Jack Armstrong got off his horse and swaggered into the store. "You Abe Lincoln?" he asked.

"That's me," Abe replied.

"Ha," Jack Armstrong said. "You're as long as a rail, I'll give you that. But you're far too skinny to be any use in a wrestling match."

"You think so?" Abe said. "Is that a challenge?"

"If you think you're up to it," Jack replied as he turned to walk out. "I'll meet you at dusk on the bluff."

As the day progressed, it seemed as though the whole town heard about the challenge. Many people came into the store to offer Abe advice or to wish him luck. Abe closed the store at 4 P.M. and made his way to the bluff that overlooked the river. A crowd had already gathered there.

When Abe arrived, the Clary's Grove boys closed ranks around Jack Armstrong. "Ready?" one of them asked Abe.

Abe nodded, stripped off his shirt, and stood ready.

People whom Abe knew well stood around discussing who they thought would win the fight and betting knives and trinkets on their picks.

Soon Abe and Jack Armstrong faced each other. While Abe was a good five inches taller than his opponent, Jack was barrel-chested and much heavier. As soon as the two men touched, the crowd began to roar. Abe grabbed Jack around the shoulders and tried to pull him toward the ground, but Jack managed to break free and instead grabbed Abe around the waist and pulled him to the ground. Dust flew into the air as the two men writhed, each trying to get the upper hand and subdue the other. Neither man would give in.

Jack proved to be a much tougher opponent than the men who had tried to rob the boat near Madame Duchesne's plantation in Louisiana two and a half years before. Finally, though, Abe was able to wriggle free and jump to his feet. Jack bounced to his feet, too. Sweat dripped off both men.

The two of them circled each other, looking for the right opportunity to strike again. As Jack turned, the edge of his right boot dragged in the dust, throwing him slightly off balance for a split second. It was all the advantage Abe needed. He lunged forward, wrapping his arms around his opponent, immobilizing him and knocking him backward onto the ground. Abe followed him down, landing his full weight on Jack's chest and pinning his shoulders into the dust.

Before Abe could catch his breath and ask his opponent if he wanted to concede, five of the Clary's Grove boys had piled on top of him and tried to drag him off their leader. Somehow Abe managed to squirm his way free, scramble to his feet, and back away from the fight. He held up his hands. "I'll challenge any one of you to the contest of your choice—running, fighting, or wrestling—" he said, "but there's no fairness in the five of you taking me on at once. What do you say?"

The crowd stopped roaring and waited quietly to see what the Clary's Grove boys' next move was. The men picked themselves up off the dusty ground, but before they could do anything, Jack Armstrong, wiping blood from the corner of his eye, walked over to Abe. "A win's a win," he said, reaching out his hand to shake Abe's.

Abe reached out and shook Jack's hand. "A good fight," he said, making no reference to the way it had ended. The two men quickly became friends.

One day in the spring of 1832, Bowling Green stopped by the store with a startling proposition for Abe. "Why don't you run for state legislator?" he asked. "We need someone in Vandalia to represent our needs."

Abe put down the corn he was weighing and stared at the justice of the peace. "Run for state legislator?" he repeated to make sure he had heard right.

At first the idea seemed outrageous. Abe thought back to his childhood in Kentucky, when he had watched well-dressed politicians clad in beaver hats and neatly pressed jackets on their way to Louisville. He certainly did not fit the bill. He was not from a wealthy family, and he had no friends in high places.

Still, the more Abe thought about running for political office, the more he liked the idea. Why shouldn't an ordinary person have his say in how the state was governed? New Salem faced the challenge of getting money to widen the river so that steamboats could come all the way up to the town, bringing cargoes of salt, iron, and manufactured goods and carrying farm produce back downstream. In the legislature Abe could fight for this. He could also fight against some government officials' suggestion of building a railroad from the Illinois River to Springfield, bypassing New Salem altogether and making it all but impossible for local farmers to compete against those with railroad access. There was no doubt about it: New Salem needed its own voice in Vandalia, the state capital. And Abe began to think he might be capable of doing the job.

Finally Abraham Lincoln announced himself as a candidate for the state legislature. He did not run under any party's banner. It was a strange time for American politics. The old Federalist party was breaking down, and individual leaders with no party affiliations were stepping forward. They included men like Andrew Jackson, John Quincy Adams, and Henry Clay. Abe was particularly impressed with Clay's ideas.

Now it was time for Abe to write down his thoughts on a number of issues that would form the platform for his campaign. He thought long and hard about what he wanted to stand for. He thought about the people in New Salem who had stopped by the store to buy groceries and tell him their problems and troubles. Abe asked himself what would make their lives better. And when he had decided what that was, he wrote an article for the *Sangamon Journal*, a Springfield newspaper. In the article he declared that if elected he would support any measure in the legislature, such as making the river more navigable for steamboats, that benefited New Salem and surrounding Sangamon County.

Next he outlined one of his favorite topics, the idea of free education for all children. He wrote: "That every man may receive at least a moderate education and thereby be enabled to read the histories of his own and other countries, by which he may duly appreciate the value of our free institutions, appears to be an object of vital importance, even on this account alone, to say nothing of the advantages and satisfaction to be derived from all being able to read the Scriptures and other works, both of a religious and a moral nature, for themselves."

Thirdly, he dealt with reducing the amount of interest a moneylender was allowed to charge a client. This was important to Abe because he had seen several men in New Salem ruined by their desperate need to borrow money at such high rates of interest that they had no hope of paying it back.

Abe's platform concluded with these words. "I was born and have ever remained in the most humble walks of life. I have no wealthy or popular relations to recommend me.... If the good people in their wisdom shall see fit to keep me in the background, I have been too familiar with disappointments to be very much chagrined." In other words, if he did not get elected, he would not be too disappointed. He'd had so many setbacks in his life that one more would not worry him greatly.

Although Abe wrote that he would not be too upset if he did not get voted into the state legislature, his personal circumstances were pointing toward the need to find a new job soon. Abe had found out too late that Denton Offutt was much too ambitious. Instead of being content with the steady income the store brought in, Denton had bought a large number of hogs to sell downriver. Sadly, the deal had gone bad, and Denton could no longer afford to keep the store open.

Then one morning in April 1832, as Abe pondered what to do about a job, a man rode into town and posted a notice that read, "Needed by order of Governor John Reynolds, 400 volunteers of sound mind and body to sign up for the Sangamon County state militia for a period of thirty days."

Abe read the notice thoughtfully. He had been waiting for something like this to happen. On April 6, Black Hawk had crossed the Mississippi River into Illinois with 368 warriors, about 1,000 women and children, and 450 horses. Black Hawk, the sixty-seven-year-old leader of the Sauk and Fox Indian tribes, said his people had returned to their traditional lands to plant corn, but no one believed him. The local residents thought he was after revenge. This was because he claimed he had been tricked into signing away his tribal lands. The white men had given the Indian leaders a lot of alcohol to drink and then settled deals with them. In their drunken state, Black Hawk and the other leaders had agreed to relocate their tribes farther west. But now the Indians were back!

Abe decided to sign up for the militia. He borrowed a horse from a friend and rode to Richmond Creek to join the rest of the ragtag troops. When he arrived, he was not surprised to find that the Clary's Grove boys had beaten him there.

A captain for the militia needed to be chosen, and this was done in a unique way. The men were allowed to shout out the name of someone they thought would make a good leader. Two names were put forward: Bill Kirkpatrick and Abraham Lincoln. The two men stepped forward, and then the rest of the men fell in line behind the man they wanted to be their captain.

Abe stood nervously while the men got in line. He had never been nominated to lead anything before. When he turned around, he saw that the line behind him was twice as long as the line behind Bill Kirkpatrick.

The newly appointed Captain Lincoln chose Jack Armstrong, the man he had wrestled six months earlier, to be his sergeant. Within an hour the militia was marching to Beardstown to join up with sixteen hundred other soldiers amassing there.

The job of keeping the company of men moving in the right direction in close formation and without fighting proved a big challenge to Abe and Jack. Few of the men had been in the army before, and the men soon grew tired of marching and setting up camp. Although Abe tried to act like a real captain, he hardly knew what was expected of him in the role.

Several days into the march, the company was crossing a field when Abe noticed they were approaching a fence with a narrow gate in it. The men were marching in lines twenty wide, and there was no way they could go through the gate unless they regrouped into rows of two or three abreast. The trouble was, Abe didn't know what order to give to have his men change formation. He tried to think of an alternative. Suddenly the answer came to him. "Halt!" he ordered. "This company will break ranks and re-form in two minutes on the other side of the gate."

The soldiers were glad for the quick break and did not suspect that the reason for it was to save Abe the embarrassment of having to admit he didn't know the necessary commands to keep them moving through obstacles in close formation.

Finally, on April 25, the troops arrived at Beardstown and joined the ranks of the other assembled soldiers. Abe was given corn, pork, flour, and whiskey to feed his men. The next day the men were issued muskets and bayonets and told to march toward Yellow Bank (now called Oquawka). The force of men set a good pace, covering between twenty and twenty-five miles a day on this march.

Once the soldiers arrived at Yellow Bank, they had no rest. They marched another twenty-five miles to reach Dixon Ferry near Prophetstown. This part of the march was much more difficult as they pushed and heaved loaded supply wagons through the swampy undergrowth.

By the time they reached the ferry, most of Abe's men had had enough. They had not been able to find dry wood for a fire and had resorted to eating raw pork. And with so much walking, their boots had holes in them. As well, arguments soon erupted between groups of militiamen from different counties.

At Dixon Ferry another company of men was waiting to join them, but there were no orders on how they should proceed from there. Abe hoped that orders would come soon, before things got too out of hand among the men. The new company of soldiers that joined them, however, were even more bored and disgruntled than Abe's men. They had come to fight Indians and would not be satisfied until they had found some to fight.

Chapter 9

Doing Something Useful

The only good Indian is a dead Indian," Captain Abraham Lincoln heard someone yell. He hurried toward the commotion, every sense on high alert. As he rounded a tent, he saw a group of men from his company and from the company led by Major Stillman clustered in a circle. He could see over their heads to the middle of the group, where an old Indian man stood clutching a piece of paper.

"It's a letter from General Cass," Abe heard the Indian say, his eyes wide with fear.

"A letter!" laughed one of the Clary's Grove boys. "How's a letter going to protect you?"

"Let's get him!" yelled another man.

Abe elbowed his way to the front. He took the letter from the old Indian and quickly read it. "This man is right," he told the group. "He has a letter allowing him to be in the area. He means us no harm."

A shout of rage went up from the soldiers. "I enlisted to kill Indians, and here's an Indian. He's not getting out of here alive."

Abe knew he had only a second to decide what to do. Determined not to just leave the soldiers to vent their rage on the Indian, Abe pushed the old man behind him. "Whoever wants to harm him will have to kill me first," he vowed, looking the men under his command in the eye.

Abe saw rage in their faces, then resignation. He seized the moment. "Go on back to what you were doing," he ordered. "I'll take care of our visitor."

Slowly the men drifted away, and Abe escorted the Indian safely out of the camp and watched as he disappeared into the woods.

As he walked back to camp, Abe worried about the men. They were spoiling for a fight, and he knew that when someone wants a fight, he usually finds one. He decided to keep his company extra busy with chores until they were on the move again.

That night, though, Abe's fears came true. His blood ran cold when he heard what had happened. Some of the soldiers had seen Indians on horseback about a mile from camp. Instead of alerting their commander, several of Major Stillman's men had decided to go off on their own "Indian hunt." They grabbed their rifles and headed off into the moonlit night. Thankfully, Abe's men were too loyal to him to go off without orders.

The men from Major Stillman's company found the Indians, and what they were looking for—a fight. But when it was over, twelve soldiers lay dead, each scalped and stripped of his weapons.

It was a gruesome sight that Abe and his men confronted the following morning when they came to bury the bodies. As they silently went about the grisly task, Abe recognized several of the dead soldiers. They had been in the forefront of the efforts to kill the old Indian with the letter. Abe consoled himself with the thought that his men had not disobeyed his command. He hoped to be able to send each man in his company home in one piece when their stint in the militia was up.

Abe was glad when the order came for his company to start moving again. The men were easier to handle when they were exhausted from a hard day of marching. And they marched all the way to Lake Koshkonong in southern Wisconsin. As they marched, they kept a lookout for Black Hawk and his men, but they saw no sign of them. All they found were mosquitoes that made life miserable by biting them through the worn holes in their clothes. To make matters worse, their tents leaked when it rained.

Abraham Lincoln and his company of militiamen were finally discharged on July 10, 1832, after eighty days of service.

It should have been a fast trip home following the discharge, but someone stole two horses the night before they were to set out. One of the stolen horses belonged to Abe and the other to another man from New Salem. However, Abe's men came to the rescue. Instead of riding off, they all traveled together, taking turns riding the remaining horses and walking.

When they reached Peoria, Abe and the other man made a canoe. As they paddled it downriver to New Salem, Abe calculated how much money he had made serving in the militia. He put the figure at around one hundred twenty-five dollars, though he knew it would be weeks, perhaps even months, before he saw any of the money. The army paymaster would bring it to him in New Salem in due course. The first thing Abe had to do with the money when it arrived was pay for the stolen horse he had borrowed from his friend.

Abe had received something more important than money from his experience in the militia. He had a new pride in his ability to lead other men. And in the process of leading the men, he had rubbed shoulders with all sorts of people, learning something from each of them. In particular, he learned a lot from two lawyers who had served under him, Orville Hickman Browning and John Todd Stuart.

Once back in New Salem, Abe had a lot to do if he was going to get elected to the state legislature in eighteen days. He had very little money to do it with, certainly not enough to buy a new set of clothes to campaign in. Instead, he made do with what he had. He set off into the countryside wearing a threadbare coat with tails that were so short he could not sit on them and a pair of rough linen pants that were too short for his gangly frame, stopping halfway down his shins. As well, he wore a straw hat and the boots he had used in the militia.

Certainly there was nothing inviting about the way Abe looked, but as soon as he opened his mouth to speak, people stopped to listen. Abe had a never-ending supply of jokes and stories that he told to the delighted voters. When he had warmed up an audience with his homespun banter, he would slip in some of his political ideas. He made friends wherever he went, and just about everyone he met promised to vote for him.

On Election Day the people kept their promise, and 277 of the 300 votes cast in the New Salem precinct went to Abraham Lincoln. However, voters outside the area had not heard of Abe and so did not vote for him. As a result Abe came in eighth out of thirteen candidates. Since only the top four candidates got to go to the state legislature, Abe was once again without a job or a direction for his life.

Abe seriously considered becoming a blacksmith. He was strong enough to easily handle the work, but in the end, he decided he didn't want to spend the rest of his life shaping metal.

Finally the opportunity to own a half share of a general store presented itself. Abe was glad to take up the opportunity, especially since the current owner of the store was prepared to let him make payments on the business. Once again, Abe, along with his new partner Bill Berry, who had served under him in the militia, settled into tending shop.

Abe and Bill sold a wide range of merchandise in the store, everything from tea, coffee, sugar, and salt to brown muslin, blue calico, and men's and women's hats and shoes. Times were starting to get tough around New Salem, though, and the store did not prosper the way its new owners had hoped it would.

The store did, however, give Abe a roof over his head and the chance to do the two things he liked best: talk to passersby and read books. He particularly enjoyed poetry and memorized several long poems, including *Tam o'Shanter* and *The Cotter's Saturday Night,* both by Robert Burns, and Oliver Wendell Holmes's *The Last Leaf.* Abe learned that a farmer who lived six miles away had a copy of Kirkham's *English Grammar,* from which he also set about memorizing pages.

After about six months of running the store, Abe and Bill had to admit they were losing money fast. Without improvements on the river, farmers around New Salem had no cheap, reliable way to get their produce to market. As a result they had little money to spend at the store.

In early spring 1833, Abe closed the doors of the store for the last time and began the now familiar job of searching for work. He split fence rails for a while and also worked as a clerk. But neither of these jobs paid much, and soon Abe was convinced he would have to go farther afield to find work.

Abe's many friends in New Salem did not want to see him leave. They got together and decided he was perfect for the job of postmaster. The present postmaster, Samuel Hill, also owned a store that sold alcohol. People trying to mail letters complained that he ignored them in favor of customers who came in to buy whiskey. On May 7, 1833, Samuel Hill resigned as postmaster, and Abraham Lincoln took over the job.

The pay was not good, around fifty dollars a year, but Abe was glad to have the job. Once again, it put him in touch with everyday people and provided plenty of reading material. As postmaster, Abe was not only entitled to receive mail free of charge but also had time to read any newspaper that came through his office.

Abe's main jobs were receiving and franking mail to be sent out and calculating the postage due on incoming letters. The mail arrived by a post rider twice a week unless he was held up by bad weather or an injured horse. Each arriving letter was folded and sealed with wax. It was Abe's job to count the number of sheets of paper each letter contained and read the postmark that told where it had been sent from. With this information he figured out how much the person receiving the letter needed to pay in postage. In 1833 the person mailing a letter did not pay the cost of sending it; the person receiving it did. And it was not cheap to receive a letter. It cost six cents for a single sheet of paper to be sent thirty miles.

Abe loved to walk in the woods, and he often stuck letters under his hat and hand-delivered them to farms as far away as six miles during his walks. Although hand delivery was not part of the job, he liked to offer the best possible service he could.

Except for the wages, being postmaster was an ideal job for Abe. He was five hundred dollars in debt from the failed general store and needed to start paying the money back. Once again Abe's friends came to the rescue, suggesting that Abe become a surveyor in his spare time. Abe liked the idea. He still recalled the way his father had had to leave the farm in Kentucky because of boundary disputes. Even the legendary Daniel Boone had lost most of his land the same way. The only way to avoid such situations in the future was to make sure land was properly surveyed.

There was just one problem with becoming a surveyor—Abe had no idea how to go about survey-ing a piece of land. Still, he determined that this was what he wanted to do and set about acquiring the new skill he needed. He sent for two books, one on surveying and the other on geometry and trigonometry. As soon as they arrived, he devoted every spare moment to studying them. Sometimes Abe stayed up all night reading the books in the flickering firelight.

His hard work and study paid off six weeks later when Abe was ready to begin surveying. He bor-rowed money to buy a horse, a saddle, and a bridle, as well as a chain and compass. John Calhoun, the county surveyor, was glad to hand over part of his "territory" to Abe. Many people were settling on the flat prairie that stretched out behind New Salem, and there was enough work to keep both surveyors busy. Every new farm and hamlet in the area had to be surveyed and the boundaries of the various properties pegged. Abe worked hard. He surveyed the towns of Petersburg, Bath, New Boston, Huron, and Albany and many 160-acre lots and country roads.

While Abe was out surveying the countryside, he began thinking about running for the state legislature again. Elections were to be held in August 1834.

Abe had learned some lessons from his failure in the previous election, and he was determined to do everything he could to win this time. He decided not to make long political speeches or to publish his platform in the newspaper. Instead he asked everyone he knew to vote for him. And by now, as a result of his serving in the militia, being postmaster, and surveying land, Abraham Lincoln knew a lot of people.

Unlike the last election, by 1834 two distinct political parties were emerging: the Democratic Party, headed by President Andrew Jackson, and the Whigs, who followed Henry Clay. Abe, of course, preferred the Whigs, though he did not come out and say so openly. He had to walk a narrow line. Most people in New Salem were Whigs, while the farmers in the surrounding countryside tended to be Democrats, and Abe needed all of their votes.

John Todd Stuart, the Springfield lawyer who had served under Abe during the Black Hawk War, was already in the state legislature. He served as the leader of the Whigs, and he helped Abe to campaign wisely and understand the political process. On August 4, 1834, when all the votes had been tallied, Abraham Lincoln gained 1,376 votes, coming in second in the election and securing a seat in the legislature.

The next session of the state legislature was not scheduled to begin until November, so Abe continued on as postmaster and surveyor in New Salem. Beside this, however, as well as being a newly elected state legislator, Abe had another focus. John Todd Stuart had rekindled Abe's interest in the law, but this time Abe didn't just want to observe cases being heard before a justice of the peace. He wanted to become a lawyer himself. This involved studying a long list of law books and taking an examination.

His friendship with John Todd Stuart gave Abe the confidence he needed to forge ahead with this new venture. Whenever he had a spare moment, Abe picked up one of the law books his friend had loaned him and read it. Indeed, some of the local people began to accuse him of being lazy, since all he seemed to do these days was read. They found it hard to understand why a strong man like Abraham Lincoln would want to study law when he could be out in the fresh air doing something useful!

Finally November rolled around. Abe borrowed some money from a friend and spent sixty dollars of it buying his first-ever tailor-made suit. He also bought himself one of the new fashionable stovepipe hats some of the men were now wearing. He

then packed his few belongings into a bag and
caught the stagecoach to Vandalia, the state capital. As he looked out the window on that gray afternoon, he wondered what lay ahead for him. Would
he be a good state legislator? Would he do and say
the right things in the presence of so many educated people? And would he eventually pass the
bar exam and become a lawyer? Abe, who'd had
less than a year of formal education, had serious
doubts about all of these concerns. He was about
to find out for sure.

Chapter 10

A Chance to Prove Himself

"Call to order. The legislature is now in session." With these words Abraham Lincoln found himself sitting among fifty-five other state representatives and twenty-six senators. The date was December 1, 1834, and everyone was seated behind tables in a large hall that had a fireplace on one side and a stove on the other. The men sat three to a table, and the Speaker of the House sat alone on a platform at the front of the hall. Spittoons were placed around the room for convenience, and there was a pail of water with three tin dippers for the men to drink from.

Even though Abe was the second youngest representative in the State House, he was surprised that he didn't feel out of place. Over half of the other representatives were farmers. A number of them were also inexperienced with state government, and several had less education, though Abe did not advertise how little schooling he'd actually had!

Abe decided to listen carefully to the proceedings at first and learn how things worked in the legislature. Only then would he venture out and make speeches on his own. The plan worked well, and since Abe was rooming with John Todd Stuart, he had many opportunities to meet with prominent members of the legislature outside of formal meetings.

For the most part, business at the Capitol amounted to small dealings: granting rights for ferry crossings, issuing divorce decrees, setting aside money to survey government land, and ordering that the stovepipe in the hall be replaced. The two big issues of the day were authorizing and paying for a canal to connect the Illinois River with Lake Michigan so that cargo could travel by boat all the way from the Atlantic Ocean into the interior of Illinois and chartering a state bank so that farmers and developers would have access to money to help develop the unbroken land to the West.

Abe found some of this fascinating and some of it boring, although he never missed a meeting of the legislature. John Todd Stuart had his sights set on moving up to the United States Congress, and slowly he began grooming Abe to take his place as a Whig leader.

Abe's two-year term in Vandalia passed quickly. At the end of March 1836, he returned home to

New Salem. He had a pile of new stories to tell and a determination to get reelected. He was also determined to take the law exam and become a lawyer. On September 9, 1836, Abe gathered up his courage and took the examination in Springfield. He was surprised at how easy it was, and he passed with top grades. Now this self-taught farm boy could enter the courts, not as an observer, as he had done so many times in the past, but as a lawyer and active participant in the proceedings. Abe could not have been happier.

The political mood of the country was changing away from the more popular Democrats and toward the Whigs, who had been the underdogs up until this time. Many voters did not like the Democrats' new method of choosing candidates at conventions, and they swung their support toward the Whigs. Abraham Lincoln and eight other Whigs swept the election of 1836.

Abe could not wait to get back to Vandalia. The Tenth General Assembly convened on December 5, 1836, and since the assembly sat for only three months at a time, it was due to go into recess on March 8 the following year. The nine Whig members quickly became known as the "Long Nine," because they were all unusually tall. The men averaged over six feet in height, with two being even taller than Abe's six feet four inches. These men had come to Vandalia with one main objective: they wanted the state capital moved to Springfield. In their opinion, Vandalia had not been the best choice from the beginning. It was too small and isolated, and it was too far south. Central and northern Illinois were opening up to settlers, and the capital needed to be nearer the center of population growth.

Abe led the charge. It was a bitter fight, with many representatives fighting hard to keep Vandalia as the state capital. In the end, Abe proposed that if Springfield would be willing to donate fifty thousand dollars to relocate the legislature and two acres of land on which to build a new State House, they would move. The citizens of Springfield readily agreed, and their city became the new capital of Illinois.

When the matter of the new capital had been settled, Abe returned to New Salem to say farewell to the town where he had so many good memories. By now it was obvious to all that New Salem was a dying community. Making the river more navigable had proved impossible. With no viable way to ship their produce to market, farmers began to leave the area. And as they left, businesses in town began to close. Abe had decided it was time for him to be moving on as well. Now that Abe was a qualified lawyer, John Todd Stuart had arranged for him to join his law practice in Springfield.

On April 15, 1837, twenty-eight-year-old Abe Lincoln rode into Springfield, everything he owned stuffed into two saddlebags that hung over the rump of his horse. With a population of fourteen hundred, Springfield was the largest town Abe had ever lived in. It was also the muddiest. Springfield was a hub of trade, and a steady parade of horses and wagons laden with corn, potatoes, turnips, and wheat passed through town. As a result of this traffic, the streets, which had started out as little more than overgrown dirt tracks, quickly turned into a sea of mud. This circumstance particularly suited the hogs that were herded through town on their way to market. Inevitably some escaped, and there was always a stray pig or two rooting around in the muck.

Abe stopped in front of Joshua Speed's general store, tied up his horse, and strolled inside. "How much is a mattress for a single bed, sheets, and a pillow?" he asked, planning to buy the items and take them down the street to a boardinghouse.

Joshua scribbled some figures on a piece of paper and then looked up. "That would be seventeen dollars," he replied.

Abe gulped. "I have no doubt that's a fair price, but I do not have that kind of money right now. If you would give me credit until Christmas and my experiment at being a lawyer here works out, I will be able to pay you in full. But if it fails, I can't say when I would be able to pay you."

Joshua looked at Abe for a moment before speaking. "You're that Abe Lincoln who got Springfield made the capital, aren't you?"

Abe nodded. "That's me."

"I'll tell you what," Joshua said. "If you need somewhere to stay, I have a big bedroom upstairs. You can share the room with me if you like. Let's not worry about money for now; it won't cost me anything for you to stay."

Abe could hardly believe his good fortune. He did not want the opportunity to slip away, so he quickly asked, "Where's your room?"

"Up the stairs on the right," came the reply.

Abe rushed outside to get his saddlebags. He bounded up the stairs two at a time and deposited the saddlebags on the bedroom floor. He was back downstairs within a minute. "I'm all moved in," he laughed. "Now I must see my new place of business."

Abe had visited John Todd Stuart's office several times before but never dreamed he would one day be working there. The office itself was a humble affair, a single room conveniently located above the circuit courtroom on Hoffman's Row.

When Abe arrived at the office, the first thing he noticed was the freshly painted sign above the door that read "Stuart & Lincoln." He paused to admire it for a moment. This was one of the proudest moments in his life. He wished his mother and Sarah could have seen it. He was a partner in a law firm, albeit the junior partner, but a partner nonetheless. Abe could scarcely believe it, and he suspected that those who had known him growing up in Little Pigeon Creek back in Indiana would have a hard time believing it, too.

Inside, John Todd Stuart greeted Abe warmly. Abe hung up his coat and looked around. The room had not changed, except that another high-backed chair had been brought in. Other than that, it was the same old woodstove in the corner, the same bookshelves, table, chairs, and bench for clients to sit on. And the same buffalo hide was draped over one of the chairs. The office was not fancy, but Abe didn't mind; all he wanted was a chance to prove himself.

Abe did not have to wait long. The law firm handled cases from land deed disputes to defending people charged with everything from trespassing to murder. John Todd Stuart was swamped with work, and Abe soon had his first big case. He defended William Fraim, who was charged with killing a farmhand in a drunken brawl. Abe did the best he could, but there was little to be said in Fraim's defense. Fraim's crime had been witnessed by a number of people. Abe lost the case, and William Fraim was hanged.

In another case, Abe defended Henry Truett. Truett and another man, Jacob Early, had a long-standing feud that came to the boiling point one evening in the parlor of the Spottswood Hotel. Henry Truett drew a pistol, and Jacob Early picked up a chair. At this, Truett raised the gun and shot Early dead. It was a sensational case, and Henry Truett was indicted for murder. In court Abe argued that when Jacob Early picked up the chair, he had, in fact, picked up a "deadly" weapon. This action caused Henry Truett to fear for his life. As a result, he shot Jacob Early in self-defense. Of course, the other way to look at the events was to say that Early had picked up the chair in self-defense because he was afraid of Truett, who had drawn a pistol.

Abe spent many hours preparing his closing argument to the jury. It was a stirring summation of the case delivered with his usual homespun charm and forthrightness. And in the end it swayed the jury, who returned a verdict of not guilty. Henry Truett went free, and around town Abe's reputation as a lawyer began to grow.

While Abe was settling into his new career, an old problem was simmering in the background— slavery. In October 1837 the Reverend Mr. Jeremiah Porter spoke out against slavery. He was part of an abolitionist group who wanted to see slavery done away with and all black people set free. The meeting turned into a mob scene, and Mr. Porter was lucky to get out of town with his life. A week later Judge Thomas Browne spoke to the townspeople about the court's view of slavery. He said that abolitionists were dangerous members of society who should be shunned by all good citizens.

Abraham Lincoln was appalled by these remarks. He had long ago concluded that the United States worked because it was ruled by laws based upon logical precepts and not emotion. He believed that the citizens of any free society must be able to read and speak about anything they wanted to. But now a judge was urging "good" citizens to shun people simply because they held different views. Abe could scarcely believe it. But perhaps more ominous was the fact that this was happening in an area where few black people lived. In fact, there were just seventy-eight free blacks and twenty registered indentured servants in Sangamon County. Abe wondered what catastrophes might be brewing in towns and farming communities that actually depended on slavery for their way of life. He was sure the incident with the Reverend Mr. Porter would not be the end of agitation on the question of slavery.

Abe was right. Less than a month later trouble erupted in the town of Alton, on the western boundary of the state along the Mississippi River. Elijah Lovejoy, a thirty-five-year-old abolitionist and Presbyterian minister, had moved into town. Lovejoy made it known that as soon as his printing press arrived from St. Louis he was going to start an abolitionist newspaper. The local citizens, spurred on by Judge Browne's comments, vowed not to let this happen in their town. The night the printing press arrived, it was stolen and dumped into the Mississippi. That was not the end of the matter, though. Elijah Lovejoy was a stubborn man who believed passionately in setting slaves free. He ordered a second printing press, and when it arrived, he kept it under guard. On November 7, 1837, a mob stormed the warehouse where the press was being kept. They could not get inside, so instead they set the building on fire. Elijah Lovejoy rushed to the scene to save his printing press. In the process, he was shot dead by someone in the mob.

Chills ran down Abe's spine when he heard about the incident. He hoped the issue of slavery would be settled once and for all soon, but he had a terrible feeling that a lot more blood would be shed before that happened.

Not long after the incident in Alton, Abe had the opportunity to meet Elijah Lovejoy's brother Owen, who also was a pastor. At his brother's graveside, Owen had vowed to, in his words, "never forsake the cause that had been sprinkled with my brother's blood."

These events led Abe to make his first public comments on slavery in a speech he gave before the Young Men's Lyceum of Springfield in January 1838. The address was entitled "The Perpetuation of Our Political Institutions." Abe was nervous as he started in on his speech, but slowly his nervousness left him. He launched into the heart of his message, criticizing those who took the law into their own hands for any reason. He reminded his listeners that the great heroes of the American Revolution had fought for human rights, often at the cost of their own lives. He wondered aloud what they would think of American citizens roaming around in mobs, burning churches, destroying private property, and murdering their opponents. Abe ended his speech with the words, "Whenever the vicious population shall be permitted to gather...and burn churches, ravage and rob provision stores, throw printing presses into rivers, shoot editors and hang and burn obnoxious persons at pleasure and with impunity, depend on it, this Government cannot last."

The text of his speech was printed in the *Sangamon Journal*. Seeing his words laid out in the newspaper for all to read, including those who had voted for him as their representative, Abe began to wonder whether he would ever be elected to the legislature again.

Chapter 11

A Certain Woman

Abe need not have worried about how the voters would react to his comments on slavery. He was elected again and again to the state legislature, and he served with distinction.

John Todd Stuart was now serving in the United States Congress and spending most of his time in Washington, D.C. As a result, in November 1839 Abe had taken over the bulk of his partner's legal responsibilities.

One responsibility Abe had taken over was riding the circuit. The court in Springfield actually convened for only several weeks a year. The rest of the time the judges traveled through the outlying communities holding court and deciding cases. As a result, many Springfield lawyers spent a good part of their time following the judges' circuit through these communities. In the Stuart & Lincoln law partnership, John Todd Stuart had been responsible for most of the circuit riding.

Abe now found himself out following the judges from community to community. These circuits were completed once in the spring and again in the fall, and they were always festive occasions. The local people would crowd into a schoolhouse or cabin to hear the proceedings and watch their neighbors act as jurors. They especially enjoyed hearing a good story in the course of a trial, and Abe was popular, since he seemed to have a never-ending supply of such stories. He could get a jury laughing or crying faster than anyone they had observed.

As much as Abe enjoyed riding the circuit and meeting simple country folk along the way, he soon found it took up too much of his time. He had met a certain woman and wanted to spend more time in Springfield getting to know her. The woman's name was Mary Todd.

Mary was the sister-in-law of Ninian Edwards, one of the "Long Nine." The Edwardses' house was the social hub for the Whig party in Springfield. There was a continual flow of interesting and important people through the house, and many lavish parties and concerts were held there.

Abe had never been much at talking to young women. They made him feel ill at ease, and he usually escaped their company as soon as it was polite to do so. Things were different when he met Mary Todd. She was happy to do the talking for both of them, leaving Abe to listen and nod occasionally.

Abe soon found the two of them had certain things in common. Both had been born in Kentucky, and Mary's mother had died when she was six years old. But when it came to stepmothers, their stories took different turns. While Abe's stepmother had been a loving and fair woman, Mary's had been anything but. The new Mrs. Todd had taken an instant disliking to her stepchildren and made their lives difficult. And when she began having children of her own, the lot of the stepchildren grew worse, until Mary, the last stepchild at home, felt she had to flee from her father's house. She had come to live with her sister, Elizabeth Edwards, in Springfield.

There were also other ways in which Abe Lincoln and Mary Todd were very different. Mary was from one of the most well-known and powerful families in Kentucky. Her grandfather had distinguished himself in the Revolutionary War, and her father, Robert Todd, had been a captain in the War of 1812. He had also been a state senator and was now president of the Bank of Kentucky in Lexington.

Unlike most of the women Abe had known growing up, twenty-two-year-old Mary could read and write, both in English and in French. She also played music, studied drama, and loved poetry. Indeed, she had memorized some of the same Robert Burns poems as Abe. As well, Mary had an opinion on anything to do with politics. This was a particularly unusual interest for a woman in 1840 to have, since women were not even allowed to vote.

From the first time Abe met Mary, he was infatuated with her. She was short and plump and had ringleted light brown hair and bright blue eyes. The more she talked, the more Abe liked her, until in mid-December 1840 the two of them became engaged. The wedding date was set for New Year's Day 1841. Everyone was happy with the match. Mary, who was getting on in age for a bride, was delighted not to be headed toward permanent spinsterhood. Her sister Elizabeth loved planning social events and promised to make the wedding the talk of the town for years to come. Ninian Edwards was happy too. He confided in Abe that uniting a well-established and prosperous family with an up-and-coming young lawyer and politician would be advantageous for all concerned.

There was just one problem. As the wedding day approached, Abe began to panic. Questions haunted him in the night. What made him think he could afford any wife, much less one accustomed to the level of luxury Mary Todd expected? Would she really be content to live on his salary of twelve hundred dollars a year? And how well did he really know her anyway? The more he thought about these questions, the more depressed he became, until he could barely function in daily life. Abe knew he was in no shape to get married, and so he and Mary agreed to call off the wedding.

This decision only made Abe feel worse. Soon he found it hard to get out of bed in the morning. All the sad events that had happened in his life, such as his mother's and sister's deaths, mixed with his present situation to make life feel gray and depressing. Abe knew that people were talking about him, but there seemed to be nothing he could do about it. He visited the doctor, but there was little he could do either.

Slowly, bit by bit, Abe Lincoln began again to see life in bright colors. He continued with his legal work, though he decided it was time for a change. John Todd Stuart and Abe ended their partnership, and Abe entered into a new partnership with Stephen Logan. Abe knew that people had a difficult job suppressing their laughter when they saw them together. The two partners could not have been more different. While Abe was tall and lanky, Stephen Logan was a wiry little Scotsman with frizzy red hair and a high, squeaky voice. They did have one thing in common. Neither man had any sense of fashion. Logan wore an unbleached calico shirt, a baggy, patched coat, and equally worn pants. He did not own a tie, and he wore a moth-eaten fur hat in winter and a fifty-cent straw hat in summer. Of course, Abe did not care about any of this; he was interested only in how well his new senior partner practiced law. As it turned out, Stephen Logan was a very good lawyer.

Abe settled into the new law practice and began once again to enjoy group picnics, hayrides, and dances. In a small town like Springfield, it was inevitable that he would find himself at the same gatherings as Mary Todd, and when he did, Abe was surprised that he still had feelings for her. They began courting again and on November 4, 1842, were married. They told Elizabeth and Ninian Edwards about their plan only four hours before the event. Elizabeth did her best in the allotted time, baking a wedding cake and putting up a few decorations. But all in all, it was a simple ceremony.

Thirty-three-year-old Abraham Lincoln was now a married man. It had all happened so fast in the end that he barely had time to take it in. Five days after the wedding he wrote to a fellow lawyer, "Nothing new here, except my marrying, which to me, is a matter of profound wonder."

Abraham and Mary Todd Lincoln made their first home in a single room over the Globe Tavern. Their rent was four dollars a week. The room was plenty big enough for a man who had been raised in a one-room cabin in the wilderness, but it was not quite the style Mary had been used to. The couple ate in the public dining room downstairs, and for the first time in her life, Mary did not have servants or slaves to meet her every need. While the room was the most luxurious place Abe had ever lived, Mary had higher aspirations. As well, she set about trying to transform her husband into someone who looked the way a prominent lawyer should look. Each morning she made Abe stand at the door while she inspected to make sure his tie was straight, his jacket wasn't rumpled, and his hair was neatly brushed.

Abe was a man who needed a lot of time alone to think things over, and living with a wife, especially one as talkative and high-strung as Mary, was sometimes difficult for him. Although he had resented having to ride the circuit when courting Mary, he now enjoyed the quiet it afforded him.

On August 1, 1843, Mary Lincoln gave birth to a chubby, blond son, whom they named Robert Todd Lincoln. Robert's arrival signaled the need for a bigger place to live than a room above a tavern. Mary's father was impressed that they had named their first child after him, and he came to visit. When he saw where Abe and Mary were living, he gave them the fifteen hundred dollars they needed to buy a plain frame house. The house was located southeast of the main business district in one of the more modest areas of town, but it gave them the living space they needed.

Owning a house in town was a very different experience for Abe. He took care of all the outdoor chores. He groomed and stabled his horse, milked the cow that was kept in the backyard, and chopped and carried firewood into the house. He didn't mind doing any of these chores. In fact, he had done them so many times since childhood that he could do them with his eyes closed. Mary, however, was startled by just how much work running a house involved. It was her job to pump the water from the well in the yard, cook, clean, wash clothes, and scrub the floors. She also had to keep the fire in the woodstove burning, as well as make all of her and Robert's clothes. It was quite a work-load for a woman who up until this time had done nothing more than read, dance, play music, and socialize during the day. Mary's father sent her money on a regular basis, and with it she would hire a maid—that is, if she could find one. Mary suffered from frequent headaches and often ranted at the "wild Irish lassies" she hired. No maid stayed employed in the Lincoln home for more than a few weeks. And word eventually got around to potential maids to steer clear of Mary Lincoln.

In 1844 Abe's law partner, Stephen Logan, wanted to take on his son as a legal partner and asked Abe to step aside. This was a relief to Abe, who had tired of being the junior partner, always running the errands and doing the boring paper-work. He was eager for a different arrangement and began looking around for a junior partner of his own. He decided on William "Billy" Herndon.

Abe had known Billy from the time he arrived in Springfield and boarded at Joshua Speed's general store. Billy had been the store clerk and eventually came to stay in the room with Abe and Joshua. Billy and Abe had spent many hours together laughing and talking. Like Abe, Billy Herndon had a story to tell on every topic. He also drank heavily and was in the midst of a running feud with Mary Lincoln, but Abe decided to give him a chance. He saw promise in the twenty-five-year-old and felt he had a good chance at shaping Billy Herndon into a fine lawyer.

Abe also hoped his new partner would be a good bookkeeper, since Abe himself was too easily distracted to keep accurate records of how much money he had made and from whom. For the first few months all went well, and then Billy Herndon slipped into the same bad record-keeping habits as Abe had. Eventually the two of them came to an agreement. Any money they got from legal work would be split fifty-fifty as soon as it was received. This approach kept the need for bookkeeping to a minimum.

In spring 1846 Mary and Abe's second child, a son whom they named Edward (Eddie for short), was born.

Despite his busy legal practice and growing family, Abe never lost sight of a goal he had set for himself. He wanted to become a United States congressman. In 1846 he set out to make this dream a reality. It was a hard-fought battle. Abe had two opponents: Peter Cartwright, a circuit-riding minister who was standing for the Democratic party, and John Hardin, who was running against Abe to be the Whig candidate. John Hardin had already served a two-year term in the House of Representatives and hoped to enjoy at least another term. Indeed, he had served the district well, and there was little reason for the voters to want him gone. However, if Abraham Lincoln was to take his place, he had to go.

Abe settled on a campaign of fairness. He had worked long and hard for the Whig party and believed he deserved a chance to go to Washington and serve in the Congress. His slogan became "Turnabout is fair play." Everywhere he went, he campaigned. Just about everyone in Springfield and the surrounding countryside knew and, for the most part, liked Abe. Some had watched him arguing cases before the court. Others had swapped stories with him in overcrowded inns and eating houses while he was out riding the circuit. So it was no surprise to many when Abraham Lincoln was chosen as the Whig candidate.

On Election Day, August 3, 1846, Abe waited anxiously as the votes were tallied to see whether he had won over his Democratic opponent.

Chapter 12

A Representative from Illinois

Abraham Lincoln won the election. He was on his way to Washington, D.C., to serve in the Congress as a representative from Illinois, one of twenty-nine states that made up the Union.

By now baby Edward was several months old and was not doing well. Abe and Mary had hoped for a strong child who could be a playmate for Robert. Instead Edward was weak and sickly. To add to this burden, Abe often came home at night to find Mary in tears, exhausted from housework and a lack of adult company.

Few wives went with their husbands to Washington when they were elected to government, but Mary Lincoln made it clear she was not going to be left alone in Springfield. If Abe was going to Washington, so was she. They had plenty of time to pack for the move, since there was more than a year's lag between being elected and taking one's seat in the House of Representatives.

In preparation for moving to Washington, Abe set about helping Billy Herndon take over full responsibility for the law firm.

Finally, on a cool day in late October 1847, the Lincoln family settled themselves into a stagecoach to start the sixteen-hundred-mile journey to Washington, D.C. The first leg of their journey took them to Alton, Illinois. Almost immediately Edward began crying, and Robert clambered up onto his father's lap and yelled at the people he saw out the window. Several other passengers on the stagecoach rolled their eyes, but Abe did not pay attention to his children's behavior. He and Mary both believed that young children were best raised without too much "interference" from their parents. Abe rarely if ever disciplined the children in any way.

"What happens when we get off the stagecoach?" Robert asked his father.

"We'll be getting on a river steamer and going all the way to St. Louis, and then we'll get on another steamer and go downriver to Cairo," Abe replied, smiling as he watched his oldest son's eyes grow wide with anticipation. "And then the steamer is going to take us up the Ohio River to Carrollton, and then down the Kentucky River to Frankfort."

"And what about the train? When do we take the train?"

"When we get to Frankfort," Abe replied patiently, "we'll get the train to Lexington. That's where we're going to stay with Mother's family."

"How many nights will it take to get there?" Robert continued with his questions.

"Oh, about ten days. It's a long way," Abe replied, looking out the window at the wide-open Illinois countryside.

Soon Abe was engulfed in his own world, thinking about what lay ahead for him in Washington. This was not an easy time to be headed to Congress. It was over a year and a half ago now that President James Polk, a Democrat, had made clear his view on Mexico's right to disputed land. Abe had read Polk's words so many times he had them memorized. "Mexico has passed the boundary of the United States, has invaded our territory and shed American blood upon American soil. War exists, and, notwithstanding all our efforts to avoid it, exists by the act of Mexico herself."

Abe shook his head as he thought about the pompousness of the statement. The trouble between Mexico and the United States had grown out of an argument over where the border between the two countries really lay. Texas, which had been annexed by the United States and admitted to the Union in December 1845 as the twenty-eighth state, had once been a part of Mexico. The new state claimed that its southwestern boundary went all the way to the Rio Grande, but Mexico claimed that the border was one hundred miles farther east along the Nueces River.

In Abe's opinion, President Polk had not tried hard enough to resolve the issue diplomatically before sending in troops. In battle after battle, ill-equipped Mexican soldiers had been killed and

Mexico's boundary with the United States beaten back. President Polk's treatment of California also was particularly troubling to Abe. In the past, the United States had tried to buy California and New Mexico from Mexico, but the effort had been rebuffed. Now, with Mexico in a weakened state and war declared, the United States Army had marched into California and taken it by force.

Six weeks before, on September 14, 1847, eight thousand United States troops led by General Winfield Scott had overrun Mexico City and brought the fighting to an end. Abe knew that one of the first things that Congress would have to do would be to ratify a peace treaty. But he felt sorry for Mexico. What kind of peace was it when a stronger neighbor could invade your land and claim it as theirs at any time? Of course, this was not a popular view. Most Americans were proud of the military's efforts in capturing so much Mexican territory.

Mary Lincoln was exhausted by the time they arrived in Lexington. In contrast, Abe felt well rested, as he had an amazing ability to block out the noise and distraction his children were causing on the various forms of transport they traveled on.

This was the first time Abe had been in Lexington and the first time he had met Mary's stepmother and many of her stepbrothers and sisters. He also got to see the huge house Mary was raised in and the comfortable lifestyle she had been accustomed to. Mary's brother Levi took Abe out to the Oldham, Todd & Company cotton mills, the family business where he was assistant manager.

The lifestyle of Lexington reminded Abe of New Orleans, which he had visited sixteen years before. All the Todd family money came through businesses that used slave labor. Mary had been attended by slaves all of her life growing up. She did not find this troubling, but Abe did. Instead of enjoying the beauty and bustle of Lexington, everywhere he looked he saw people being held captive like animals.

While in Lexington, Abe heard the story of a slave named Eliza who came up for sale at a slave auction in the city. Eliza was a tall, elegant young woman who was only one-sixty-fourth black. Indeed, those who saw her told Abe she looked whiter than he did. But this did not matter, since Southern states operated on a "one drop of blood" policy, which stated that even people with only one drop of black blood in them were to be treated as black in the eyes of the law.

Two men bid for Eliza, one a young American man and the other an older Frenchman. The bidding went higher and higher, up to twelve hundred dollars before it stalled. The auctioneer thought he could do better, so he stripped Eliza naked so the men could get a better view of what they were bidding for. Eliza fainted from fear and embarrassment, but the bidding went on. Eventually, the younger man won out with a bid of $1,585.

As he heard the story, Abe felt depressed at the thought of a woman, any woman, being treated in such a way. As a result, he was caught off guard by the story's surprise ending.

When the auctioneer yelled to the young American man who had just bought Eliza, "You got a mighty fine prize here. What are you going to do with her?" the young man yelled back, "Free her!"

A gasp went through the gathered crowd. The buyer turned out to be a young Methodist pastor named Calvin Fairbanks. He was buying and freeing slaves with money donated by rich men in the North.

Of course, not everyone was thrilled to hear that slaves were being bought and freed. But the story gave Abe hope and encouragement that slavery could one day be done away with for good in the United States.

After three weeks in Lexington, Abe was ready to move on. Mary's stepmother constantly criticized the children, and Abe found it depressing to be waited on by slaves. So it was a great relief to him when the family boarded a train that would take them to Winchester, Virginia, through Harpers Ferry gorge, along the Potomac, and into Washington, D.C. The Lincoln family set foot in Washington for the first time on December 2, 1847.

After spending one night at Brown's Hotel, Abe set off in search of Mrs. Sprigg's boardinghouse, which had been recommended to him. There had been a storm overnight, and the puddles were deep and icy. Abe did his best to avoid them, along with the stray geese and pigs that careened passed him. As he walked along Pennsylvania Avenue, his hands thrust into his pockets to keep them warm, he paused for a moment to watch workmen digging holes for streetlamps. The idea of a roadway being lit at night was something new to him. Eventually Abe came to the Capitol, its wooden dome giving it an unfinished look. Beside the Capitol was a white painted building. Abe smiled to himself as he saw the sign on the front gate. Mrs. Sprigg's boardinghouse was no more than fifteen feet from the railing that ran around the Capitol grounds. The front windows of the boardinghouse overlooked the entire Capitol Park, with its bare trees standing starkly in the snow. To the left of the Capitol stood a cowshed, a reminder that Washington, D.C., was a mixture of high government and everyday life.

Abe knocked on the boardinghouse door and waited to be invited in. He was delighted to learn that there was room for his family on the second floor. Mrs. Sprigg, a bustling, efficient woman, showed him the room. It was well furnished with a bed, table, chest of drawers, and a good-sized fireplace. Abe gave the landlady a deposit and headed back to tell Mary the good news.

Later that day the Lincoln family moved into Mrs. Sprigg's boardinghouse. Abe knew it was not everything Mary had wished for, but they did not have enough money to rent a house in Washington. And Mrs. Sprigg's establishment was very close to the Capitol, where Abe would be spending most of his days.

"Are there no other women?" Mary whispered to Abe.

"I don't think so," he replied. "Mrs. Sprigg told me there are ten boarders at present, and most of them are Whig congressmen."

Abe watched his wife's face tense. Although it had been Mary's idea to come to Washington, Abe had a sinking feeling all was not going to go well.

Abe had plenty to learn as he took his place in the Congress, along with two hundred other newly elected members. One of the "oldtimers" Abe was eager to meet was John Quincy Adams, who had served as president of the United States from 1825 to 1829. Abe liked the straight-talking former president and listened to his speeches against slavery with great interest.

In Abe's opinion, the most important matter before the Congress was winding up the war with Mexico. On December 22, Abe introduced a series of resolutions calling for President Polk to explain how and why he had decided to start the war. Abe concluded his resolutions by stating that the war was "unnecessarily and unconstitutionally begun by the President of the United States."

By now the Whig party was beginning to lose its political clout, and so no one took much notice of a lone Whig congressman from Illinois. No one except the Democratic newspaper in Springfield. The editor heard about Abe's stand on the war with Mexico and branded him a traitor and a coward. Hadn't Illinois sent many of its young men off to battle? editorials questioned. People were stirred up enough to protest, and at one rally, participants expressed "deep mortification at the base, dastardly, and treasonable assault upon President Polk." Even Abe's law partner Billy Herndon argued that the United States had a right to "protect" itself, even on foreign soil. News of these events filtered back to Abe, but he did not regret saying what he said. He believed it was true and needed to be said.

At the same time this was happening, Mary Lincoln was becoming increasingly unhappy with her surroundings. One of her favorite pastimes was going to the opera or a play. Abe took her to one every month or so, but in between were weeks of grinding boredom and loneliness. On top of this, little Eddie coughed and wheezed his way through the winter, keeping his mother up at night and making it impossible for her to go out during the day. By February, Mary had had enough. She announced to Abe that a boardinghouse was no place for a family, and she was going to stay with her father in Lexington until Abe was finished in Washington.

Abe was not happy about this arrangement, but there was nothing he could do. Once Mary had made up her mind about something, that was the end of it. Sadly Abe put Mary, Robert, and Eddie on the train and waved good-bye to them, knowing he would not see them for a long while.

Time in Washington passed quickly. And now that Abe did not have a wife and sick child to worry about he was free to spend his evenings at debates or listening to lectures. His work also kept him busy, especially now that the Whigs were trying to get their man, Zachary Taylor, elected as the next president. In 1848, as Abe's term in the House of Representatives was drawing to a close, Zachary Taylor became president.

Abe's time in Washington had been a mixture of excitement and frustration. He felt he hadn't achieved much except helping President Taylor get elected. At the end of his term, Abe decided to return to Springfield and withdraw from public life.

As a result of his stand on the war with Mexico, Abe did not receive a hero's welcome when he finally arrived back in Springfield. Despite this, he found life much as it had been before he left. The family moved back into their home, which had been rented while they were away. Mary caught up on all the news from her sister, and Abe returned to his law practice. Politics in Washington had not been as fulfilling as he had imagined it would be, and he was happy to be retired from public life.

One thing had not changed since Mary had left Abe in Washington and gone to Lexington. Eddie was still sick, and finally the doctor broke the heartbreaking news that the child had tuberculosis. A pall hung over the house. Everyone knew it was only a matter of time before Eddie died.

The sad day came on February 1, 1850. The windows and balconies of the Lincoln home were draped in black bunting. Abe tried his best to console Mary, but she refused to set foot outside the front door. Eventually, Abe asked Mary's sister Elizabeth to watch over her and six-year-old Robert so that he could keep working.

It was several months before Mary finally ventured out of the house. When she did, she wore a long, black veil that covered her face. She refused to say Eddie's name and instead referred to him as her "angel boy."

Still, as Abe told his wife, life had to go on. And it did. Soon two more children, both sons, were added to the family. On December 21, 1850, Mary gave birth to William Wallace, who was named after her brother-in-law. And in April 1853, Thomas was born. He was named after Abe's father, who had recently died. The first time Abe saw Thomas, he laughed out loud at the baby's enormous head and skinny little body. "That boy looks like a tadpole!" he exclaimed. The name stuck, and Thomas was known as Tad from then on.

Abe was happy with his life. He had achieved far more than he had ever dreamed possible. He had a wife and three sons, a nice house, a good law practice, and absolutely no desire to go back into politics.

Chapter 13

A Rekindled Passion for Politics

"Come on, Father, you have to come and see. Mother says you must!" insisted eleven-year-old Robert as he yanked on Abe's arm.

Abe smiled down at his son. "All right. Lead the way," he said.

Father and son joined the throng headed for the judge's tent at the Second Annual Illinois State Fair. They walked between the rows of tables laden with jellies and jams and turned left at the pies. Mary, with Tad in her arms, was waiting for them by the handicraft section. "Look," she beamed as Abe approached, "my sister has won first place for her embroidered pillow slip."

Abe nodded and gave a weak smile as he diverted his attention to his wife and away from his thoughts about the event that had brought him to the fair. He looked at the neatly stitched cloth on the table in front of Mary, but before long, his mind was back on the upcoming event.

It was Tuesday, October 2, 1854, and everything Abraham Lincoln believed in was about to be challenged. Abe hoped he was up to the task of responding to this challenge.

"Here, this is for candy apples," he said, pulling a penny from his pocket and handing it to Robert. "Buy one each for you and Willie."

With that, Abe said to his wife, "It's almost time for the lecture. I'll see you later." He turned and walked past the row of perfectly canned goods out into the humid, overcast afternoon. Behind the tents, five thousand chairs were neatly arranged in rows in front of a podium set up for Senator Stephen Douglas, who represented Illinois in Washington, D.C. Douglas was chairman of the powerful Senate Committee on Territories.

By now most of the front seats had been taken, but Abe didn't worry. He wanted to sit near the back so that he could gauge the feeling of the audience. He found a seat and was soon lost in thought, oblivious to the festivities going on around him. As he sat thinking, a raindrop plopped onto his nose, then another onto his hand. Within minutes it was pouring, and everyone ran for shelter.

Heavy rain continued to fall, and the venue of the meeting was moved to the State House. Abe joined the throng headed there. Once everyone was inside, the smell of damp clothes was overpowering. Feeling anxious, Abe paced the hallway at the back of the building. Suddenly there was a commotion on the stairs, and the crowd parted to make way for a short, bullheaded-looking man. It was Stephen Douglas.

As the speaker made his way to the front, the room became silent. Abe could feel the tension rise. "Thank you all for coming," Douglas began. "All I ask is that you have come with an open mind and heart which seek the best for the United States of America."

Abe continued pacing in the hallway as Stephen Douglas made his case. It was hard for him to resist the urge to go to the front, jump on stage, and argue with Douglas. What was being said disturbed him greatly.

It had all begun when Stephen Douglas introduced the Kansas-Nebraska Act into Congress. This act was meant to undo the Missouri Compromise of 1820, in which Congress had decreed there would be no slave-holding states north of 36 degrees 30 minutes latitude. Most Americans, including Abraham Lincoln, accepted this compromise. Abe believed that if slavery was not allowed to spread it would eventually die out. However, the Kansas-Nebraska Act made this unlikely. The act stated that citizens of each new state should have the right to say whether their state would be a slave-holding state or not. Stephen Douglas called this idea "popular sovereignty."

In support of his act, Douglas had declared that "whenever a territory has a climate, soil, and productions making it in the interest of the inhabitants to encourage slave property, they will pass a slave code and give it encouragement. Whenever the climate, soil, and productions preclude the possibility of slavery being profitable, they will not permit it. You come right back to the principle of dollars and cents."

The Congress had argued bitterly over the new act, but on May 30, 1854, the Kansas-Nebraska Act passed into law. Its passage caused an outrage among many people in the North, and particularly in Douglas's home state of Illinois. For this reason Douglas took every opportunity to try to explain the purpose of his act.

Abe listened impatiently to Stephen Douglas's forceful speech. "I tell you, the time has not yet come when a handful of traitors in our camp can turn the great State of Illinois, with all her glorious history and traditions, into a Negro-worshiping, Negro-equality community."

A roar of approval went up from some in the crowd. Douglas thumped the podium and spoke on for three hours. Even Abe had to admit that Stephen Douglas explained the idea of popular sovereignty in such a way that it almost sounded like the best policy for all Americans, white and black.

As Douglas finished speaking, Abe knew it was time to act. There was no way Stephen Douglas would allow him on stage to express his view, so Abe climbed the stairs to the landing as the crowd began to file out of the hall. "Come tomorrow at the same time," he yelled, "and I will give a reply to

Senator Douglas's address. I will even invite him along to defend himself if he so dares."

All the next day Abe prepared his speech. He wanted to be as prepared as possible to fight for the hearts and minds of the people of Illinois.

On Wednesday night, a huge crowd packed into the hall to hear Abe's rebuttal. And Abe was ready to do battle. He took off his collar and tie, rolled up his shirtsleeves, and stepped to the podium. Stephen Douglas was sitting in the front row, his arms crossed, his mouth tightly closed, and his steely gaze fixed on Abe.

Abe pulled his speech from his pocket and unfolded it. He looked out at the sea of expectant faces, clasped his hands behind his back, leaned forward, and began in a halting voice. "As this subject is no other than part and parcel of the larger general question of domestic slavery, I wish to *make* and to *keep* the distinction between the *existing* institution and the *extension* of it so broad and so clear that no honest man can misunderstand me, and no dishonest one, successfully misrepresent me."

Abe felt his confidence rising as he spoke. It was just like being in the courtroom, except this time every person in the room was a juror who had to make up his or her own mind about what course the government should take in relation to the issue of slavery.

Next Abe carefully reviewed the history of slavery in America. He pointed out that it was Thomas Jefferson, the author of the Declaration of

Independence, who had proposed the law that said slavery should never be allowed in the northwest territories as they opened up. Abe then talked about how the Missouri Compromise had been reached and why Stephen Douglas's Act undid it. From there he went on to describe the difference between his attitudes on slavery and those of Stephen Douglas.

I cannot but hate [slavery]. I hate it because of the monstrous injustice of slavery itself. I hate it because it deprives our republican example of its just influence in the world—enables the enemies of free institutions, with plausibility, to taunt us as hypocrites—causes the real friends of freedom to doubt our sincerity, and especially because it forces so many really good men amongst ourselves into an open war with the very fundamental principles of civil liberty—criticizing the Declaration of Independence and insisting that there is no right principle of action but *self-interest.*

Before proceeding, let me say that I think I have no prejudice against the Southern people. They are just what we would be in their situation. If slavery did not now exist among us, we should not instantly give it up. This I believe of the masses north and south. Doubtless there are individuals on both sides who would not hold slaves under any circumstances, and others who would

gladly introduce slavery anew if it were out of
existence. We know that some southern men
do free their slaves, go north, and become
tip-top abolitionists, while some northern
ones go south and become most cruel slave-
masters.

Abe looked up from his notes and adjusted his
gold-rimmed reading glasses. Not a single person
in the audience moved. Relief flooded through him
as he realized they were paying rapt attention to
the complicated matters he was trying to lay out
for them. He went on.

Just application depends upon whether
a Negro is *not* or is a man. If he is *not* a man,
why in that case, he who is a man may, as a
matter of self-government, do just as he
pleases with him. But if the Negro is a man,
is it not to that extent a total destruction of
self-government to say that he too shall not
govern *himself?* When the white man governs himself and also governs *another* man,
that is *more* than self-government—that is
despotism. If the Negro is a *man*, why then
my ancient faith teaches me that "all men
are created equal" and that there can be no
moral right in connection with one man's
making a slave of another.

The room was stiflingly hot by now, and Abe
stopped to wipe his brow with his handkerchief.

Then, with a chilling hint to a possible war over slavery that Abe hoped to avoid, he continued.

> Our republican robe is soiled and trailed in the dust. Let us repurify it. Let us turn and wash it white, in the spirit, if not the blood, of the Revolution.... Let us re-adopt the Declaration of Independence and, with it, the practices and policy which harmonize with it. Let North and South—let all Americans—let all lovers of liberty every-where—join in the great and good work. If we do this, we shall not only have saved the Union, but we shall have so saved it as to make and to keep it forever worthy of the saving. We shall have so saved it that the succeeding missions of free, happy people the world over shall rise up and call us blessed, to the latest generations.

Abe paused as many people rose to their feet cheering and applauding their approval. Several women waved white handkerchiefs in support. A few people booed Abe.

The speech lasted for three hours, and when it was over Abe asked Stephen Douglas if he would like to respond to anything that he had said. Douglas climbed the stairs to the stage and set out on a two-hour speech arguing against everything Abe had just said. Abe sat quietly listening, taking mental notes on the extra points he would add to his next speech against slavery. He knew it would not be long before he clashed with Stephen Douglas again.

That night many people came to visit the Lincoln home, both to congratulate Abe and to encourage him to continue taking a stand against slavery. Their comments rekindled his passion for politics.

Other important events also happened in Springfield later that evening. Spurred on by Abe's speech, two men who were set on abolishing slavery altogether—Ichabod Codding and Owen Lovejoy—organized a meeting to set up a branch of the new Republican party in Springfield. The Republican party had formed in response to the Kansas-Nebraska Act and was committed to seeing slavery ended in all states in the United States. Twenty-six men and one boy came to the meeting. Abraham Lincoln was not one of them. He was still a staunch member of the Whig party.

In 1856 Abe was dismayed to read that Kansas had a new nickname, "Bleeding Kansas," because so much blood had been spilled there over the issue of slavery. Both antislavery Northerners and proslavery Southerners had sponsored settlers to move into the territory so that when the time to exercise popular sovereignty arrived, their side would have the most votes. Sending thousands of people into a new territory to fight over slavery was a recipe for disaster. Soon all manner of fighting broke out. Newspapers carried stories of lynchings, burnings of homes, cheating at elections, and assassinations of political figures. Tempers flared all the way to the floor of the Congress in Washington, D.C. There Senator Sumner of Massachusetts gave a rousing anti-Southern speech that made Congressman Brooks of South Carolina so angry that he attacked Sumner with a cane at the end of the speech. The two men were eventually pulled apart, but Senator Sumner was so badly beaten he almost died.

Throughout these troubled times, antislavery supporters believed that justice would eventually win over greed. That is, until the Dred Scott decision. Dred Scott was a slave from Missouri who was owned by an army surgeon. The surgeon had taken him to Illinois and then to Minnesota Territory. They then returned to Missouri. When his owner died, Dred Scott sued for his freedom because he had been taken to Northern "free" states twice by his owner. Scott argued that when he set foot on free soil he became a free man and that his owner had no right to take him back to the South and keep him as a slave. In 1857 the case made it all the way to the Supreme Court.

In deciding the case, the Supreme Court said that a black man was not and never could be a citizen of the United States, and because of this, he was not entitled to the rights given to others in the Declaration of Independence. According to the highest court in the United States, Dred Scott was nothing more than a piece of property, and as such he could be taken wherever his owner wanted to take him.

When Abe heard of the Supreme Court's decision, he set about studying every detail of it. He combed through law books and reread the Declaration of Independence along with other important documents the Founding Fathers had written. Two weeks later, he was ready to make his case to whoever would listen. He pointed out that the Declaration of Independence spoke of every man's right to "life, liberty, and the pursuit of happiness" and that nowhere did it say that black people were to be excluded from this. He urged the Supreme Court to reconsider its verdict, saying, "We think the Dred Scott decision is erroneous. We know the Court that made it has often overruled its own decisions, and we shall do what we can to have it overrule this."

Abe kept his promise. He thought about all the ways he could help the situation and decided to change parties from the Whigs, who were still trying to come up with a unified policy on slavery, to the Republicans, who were clear in their opposition to slavery.

By 1857 Abraham Lincoln was the leading person speaking out against slavery in Illinois. He also had decided to run again for political office. This time he set his sights on a position that would give him the power he needed to make a difference. Abe announced he was running for senator from Illinois. His opponent would be the sitting senator, Stephen Douglas.

Chapter 14

As Honest As He Is Shrewd

While Abe's passion for politics may have been rekindled, he still had to earn a living as he worked toward being reelected to public office. One morning in May 1858 Hannah Armstrong visited his office. Hannah was the widow of Jack Armstrong, the Clary's Grove boy Abe had wrestled back in New Salem. After the fight Abe had become good friends with Jack Armstrong and his new bride. In fact, it was Hannah who used to sew leather patches onto the knees of his pants when he was a surveyor.

"Come in, Hannah," Abe said, guiding Hannah to a plain wooden chair by his desk. "I was sorry to hear of Jack's death."

Hannah smiled politely. "He probably lived longer than his luck should have allowed. But it's Duff I've come about."

"And how is he?" Abe asked, thinking back to the dark-eyed little boy he had bounced on his knee when visiting the Armstrong home.

"He is not good," Hannah replied, slumping in the chair. "He went through a wild patch like his father, only he didn't have someone like you to keep him on the straight and narrow. He's locked up in the jail now, accused of murder."

Abe made a conscious effort to keep his voice level and calm. "Well, you had better tell me all about it."

"Duff and several of his friends were hanging around on the edge of town, drinking and picking fights. They didn't mean any real harm. You know Duff—he would never kill anyone."

Abe nodded.

"Duff says he came home and went to bed, but someone says he saw Duff hurl his slingshot at Jim Metzger. The witness says James Norris, Duff's friend, then ran over and whacked Jim Metzger in the head with a stick."

"Did the eyewitness get a clear view of their faces?" Abe asked.

Hannah Armstrong nodded glumly. "He said it was a clear moonlit night and there was no mistaking who he saw. It was Duff. After the attack, Mr. Metzger managed to climb back onto his horse and, clinging to life, made it home. His mother called for a doctor, but it was too late. He died from his injuries.

"James Norris has already been tried and sentenced to eight years in jail for his part in the attack. Duff's lawyer has managed to get the venue for the trial changed to Beardstown, but I'm afraid for Duff. I don't think his lawyer is very experienced. I couldn't stand to have Duff jailed for something he said he never did." Hannah dabbed her eyes with her handkerchief.

Abe reached out and held her hand. "Hannah, I'm glad you came to me. You know I will do all I can to help. Come home and talk with Mary while I pack some clothes. I'll go to Beardstown with you on the afternoon stagecoach."

The following morning Abe visited Duff Armstrong in the county jail in Beardstown. He went over Duff's version of the events of the night of the attack several times and then went in search of evidence.

The trial was held three days later. Abe entered the courtroom ready to defend Duff. He had a small book tucked inside his stovepipe hat and was accompanied by a farmhand.

The judge called the court to order, and trial of the case got under way. The prosecutor questioned the eyewitness, who laid out for the jury all he had seen on the night of the attack.

Finally it was Abe's turn to cross-examine. "So you are sure you saw my client?" he asked.

"Yes, sir," the witness replied. "It was bright moonlight, and I got a good look at both young men."

"You're sure?" Abe asked again.

"Yes, I'm sure," said the witness.

With that, Abe reached over the defense table and pulled out the small book inside his hat. It was the *Farmer's Almanac* for 1858. He turned to the page that showed the position of the moon on the different days of the year. "February 14," he said, looking down at the page. "Let me see. Ah, yes, on the night of the fourteenth the moon was only a quarter and setting low on the horizon. I wouldn't call that a bright moonlit night, would you?"

The witness looked confused and then turned red.

Next Abe called to the witness stand the farm-hand who had accompanied him to court. He questioned the farmhand, and it turned out he had been with Jim Metzger earlier on the evening of the attack. The farmhand told how he had watched Metzger get on his horse to head for home. Jim Metzger was very drunk, however, and had fallen off his horse several times before the two parted company. In response to Abe's questioning, the farmhand agreed that it was quite possible Jim Metzger had fallen off his horse so many times on the way home that it might look like he had been in a brawl.

Finally, Abe made a plea to the jury on behalf of Duff Armstrong. "You twelve gentlemen hold the fate of Duff Armstrong in your hands," he said. "I have known him since he was a baby, and I rocked him in his cradle many times. I knew his father before him. The Armstrongs are good people. Perhaps Duff is a little wild, much as his father was in his younger days, but he is not capable of murder. That I do know."

Abe patted Hannah Armstrong's hand reassuringly as he sat down behind the defense table.

It did not take the jury long to reach a decision. They found Duff Armstrong not guilty of murder.

News of the case and Abe's cunning use of the *Farmer's Almanac* spread quickly around the state. As a result Abe had more work than ever. However, he never lost his plan to defeat Stephen Douglas once and for all in the upcoming election.

June 16, 1858, was one of the most exciting days in Abe's life. He was at the Republican State Convention in Springfield, where he was chosen to be Illinois's Republican candidate for the Senate to run against Stephen Douglas.

Abe had worked hard for several weeks on a suitable acceptance speech for the occasion. He had written it and rewritten it, scratching out a phrase here, adding a word there. Finally, when he was satisfied with it, he had memorized it.

It was eight o'clock in the evening when Abe climbed onstage to deliver his speech. The crowd applauded and waved flags enthusiastically. When the cheering died down, Abe launched into the speech, which was about the problem of slavery. "In my opinion," he said, "it will not cease until a crisis shall have been reached and passed. 'A house divided against itself cannot stand.' I believe this government cannot endure permanently half *slave* and half *free*. I do not expect the Union to be dissolved—I do not expect the house to *fall*—but I do expect it will cease to be divided. It will become *all* one thing or *all* the other."

Abe went on to encourage all Republicans to fight slavery. "If we stand firm, we shall not fail.

Wise counsels may accelerate, or mistakes delay it, but sooner or later, the victory is sure to come."

There was more cheering and applause when Abe was finished. However, as many Republicans thought about what he had said, concerns began to grow. Did Abraham Lincoln really believe that one day the entire United States would be either slave-holding or free? Wasn't that a little too radical? Even Abe's law partner, Billy Herndon, had his doubts about the speech. "It's true," he told Abe, "but is it wise to say so?"

Abe thought it was, and he kept right on saying it.

Later that week Abe chuckled as he read an article in the newspaper that quoted Stephen Douglas's reaction to Abe's nomination. "He is as honest as he is shrewd; and if I beat him, my victory will be hard won.... He is the strong man of his party—full of wit, facts, dates—and the best stump speaker, with his droll ways and dry jokes, in the West."

Abe's first problem was attracting the kind of audience Stephen Douglas attracted. Douglas was a well-known political figure from a strong party, whereas Abe was the nominee of a struggling new political party with few contacts. Abe considered getting hold of Stephen Douglas's itinerary and following him around the state, speaking when he had finished giving his speech. However, word of this plan got out, and the Democratic newspapers made fun of Abe. "Poor, desperate creature," wrote the editor of the *Chicago Times*. "He wants an audience...[and] people won't turn out to hear him." The article went on to suggest that Abe should consider joining one of the "two very good circuses and menageries" traveling through the state "because they always attract a big crowd."

The criticism didn't bother Abe. He'd had worse things written about him, but he was still left with the problem of how to attract the same-sized crowd as his opponent. Eventually he came up with a plan that proved he was just as shrewd as Stephen Douglas had said he was. Abe challenged Stephen Douglas to a series of debates about slavery. He figured Douglas would have a hard time turning him down without looking like he was afraid to face Abe. His assessment turned out to be right. With a cheerful look on his face, though he was probably seething inside, Stephen Douglas agreed to seven debates with Abraham Lincoln.

The first debate was held in Ottawa, Illinois, and was attended by over twelve thousand people. A week later fifteen thousand attended the second debate in Freeport. Even the rain did not deter the crowd, which stood for three hours listening to what the two candidates had to say.

Onstage, the two men looked comical standing side by side. Five-foot-four-inch Stephen Douglas was stout, and the crowd nicknamed him "The Little Giant." Lanky six-foot-four Abe towered over his opponent and was called "Long Abe" or "The Tall Sucker," depending on the person's party affiliation. No matter how they looked together, people were interested in what they had to say. All of the fuss that accompanied Stephen Douglas as he rolled into town ensured that every newspaper in the area would cover the debates, which soon were dubbed the "Great Debates."

As he traveled from town to town, Stephen Douglas made sure he looked important. He hired a private railcar and traveled with his secretary, a reporter, a band, and his beautiful young wife. He often walked out onto the platform at the back of the train, smoking a cigar and sipping brandy as he waved to those lined up to see him.

Abe could not have been more different than his opponent if he had tried to be. He had no private train; Abe sat on the same bench seats as the other passengers who paid the basic train fare. Sometimes he even hitched a ride into town on an ox-drawn wagon. And instead of having his wife at his side, Mary was at home in Springfield struggling with the boys and trying to stretch the family budget now that Abe was not earning his usual income as a lawyer. And there was no secretary, no reporter, and no band following Abe.

The final debate was held in mid-October in Alton. The Sangamon-Alton Railroad ran a special excursion train at half price from Springfield, and Mary and Robert were able to accompany Abe and hear him speak.

In Alton the two men debated backward and forward in light rain. When Abe had finished, his supporters threw roses onto the platform for him. Mary gathered them up and took them back to Springfield to brighten up the house.

By this time Abe had traveled forty-two hundred miles around the state. He arrived home in time to see fifteen-year-old Robert off to Harvard University in Massachusetts.

Election Day was cold and miserable, but many people came out to vote. Abraham Lincoln won four thousand more votes than Stephen Douglas did. However, because of the way the districts were divided in Illinois, the Republicans failed to get enough delegates to make Abe Illinois's newest senator. Stephen Douglas was declared the winner of the election.

Abe was disappointed by the result, but he was glad that thousands of citizens had listened to the debates and perhaps understood the issue of slavery a little better than before. He told Billy Herndon that the campaign had given him a "hearing on the great and durable question of the age—and though I now sink out of view, and shall be forgotten, I believe I have made some marks that will tell for the cause of liberty long after I am gone."

Newspapers reported that Abe accepted defeat in "a good-natured way as any sensible man would."

Mary, however, was very upset that her husband had won the popular vote but not the election. Abe was not surprised when she went on a shopping spree to get over her disappointment. At the local haberdashery, Mary spent forty dollars buying six yards of plaid silk, ten and a half yards of cambric and cashmere, buttons, stockings, lace, and braid. She then spent thirty-eight dollars having a dress made. By the time the costs were totaled, the dress had cost enough money to feed a family of five for two months. Abe hardly noticed the new dress and did not ask her how much it cost.

Abe went back to work at his law firm but continued to look for ways to fight against the Democrats over the issue of slavery and states' rights. He made speeches in Kansas, Iowa, Ohio, Indiana, and Wisconsin during 1859. People flocked to these gatherings wanting to hear the man who had debated "the Little Giant." Abe soon found himself more popular than ever.

By January 1860 Abraham Lincoln's name was being suggested as a possible Republican candidate for president of the United States.

At first Abe would not even consider the idea. He told his friends that he did not think he was fit for such a high office. His wife thought differently. She pushed Abe to put his name forward as a candidate. And so he did.

Chapter 15

The Unexpected Winner

How are we ever going to get this place tidied up in time?" Mary Lincoln wailed as she surveyed her front room.

Abe put down the telegrams he was reading and sighed. "We'll all help," he said, eyeing Tad and Willie. "Besides, the delegation won't be arriving until the three o'clock train." He unfolded himself from his chair and began setting the dining room chairs back around the table. When he was done he called to Tad. "Come outside with me, and we'll clean off the veranda."

Tad followed his father outside. The veranda and the street beyond were a sea of ripped banners and red-white-and-blue streamers.

As Abe stooped to begin tidying the veranda, he thought about the night before. It was certainly a night he would never forget. It was considered poor taste for a candidate to attend the party convention and watch the vote, so he had been at home. It was only a few minutes after the final vote was taken on May 19, 1860, that Abe and a local newspaper editor received the news by telegram. Abraham Lincoln had emerged as the unexpected winner of the Republican nomination for president of the United States. Hannibal Hamlin, a man Abe had never met, had been voted in as his vice presidential candidate. As the news spread throughout Springfield, hundreds of people arrived at the corner of Jackson and Eighth Street, where the Lincoln house was located.

Before long the celebration had turned into a massive street party, with people pouring into town on wagons and horseback. Soon the entire house was overrun with well-wishers. It was about three in the morning before the bands had stopped playing and the scene had calmed down enough for the children to go to bed. Now Abe was expecting a group of prominent senators and congressmen from the Republican party to arrive at his home and officially offer him the candidacy.

It was well after lunch before the house was back in order, though Mary complained that it was still a long way from perfect. Abe could see that the stress of possibly being the wife of the sixteenth president of the United States was already weighing heavy on his wife.

"We have to do things the right way," Mary scolded her husband. "I have ordered ten bottles of chilled champagne to be collected by you at 2 P.M."

Abe looked down at his wife, his eyebrows raised questioningly. "Now, Mary, I have been inviting people to our home for sixteen years, and I have never offered one of them a drink of alcohol. It's my judgment that in my new position I should not change that habit."

"Don't be so stubborn," his wife snapped back. "My father would have thought it a disgrace not to offer drink to a weary traveler. These are important men, famous men, and they will be expecting a proper level of hospitality when they arrive."

"And that is what they'll get," Abe countered, "along with a large glass of cold water."

Mary swung around and stomped out of the room, slamming the door behind her. Abe looked at the boys and shrugged his shoulders. "Give her a minute or two to calm down," he said, wondering how many more tensions would come between them now that he was an important man in the Republican party and possibly the next president of the United States.

Abe was well aware that his wife came from a very different social class than he. In fact, Mary was a relative of Dolley Todd Madison, wife of James Madison, fourth president of the United States. As he filled the lamps over the mantelpiece with oil, Abe braced himself for the possibility that Mary would attempt a whole new level of "training" for him now that there was a possibility he would become president.

Abe hated arguing with his wife, especially now, when it only added to the knot he already felt in his stomach. He both welcomed and dreaded the arrival of the delegation. He had never met most of the men, but he was aware that William Seward had been the popular choice to be the presidential candidate in the first vote, though he had not received enough votes to win outright. Just about everyone attending the convention had expected Seward to eventually win the nomination. However, besides Abe, there were three other men in the race, Simon Cameron, Salmon Chase, and Edward Bate. As the votes were tallied, it was obvious that none of these three could win. One by one, Abe Lincoln's supporters encouraged the delegates who had voted for the three in the first round to switch their vote. By the third round of voting, many delegates had thrown their support behind Abe, giving him enough of a lead to be declared the winner over William Seward.

When he compared himself to William Seward, Abe had to admit he had a few shortfalls. Seward was an influential United States senator from New York. He had also served as governor of that state. The highest office Abe had ever held was one term as a congressman, and that had largely been a flop. Seward was from a wealthy and well-connected New York family and was a graduate of one of the best colleges in the country. Abe's family, who were all dead now except his stepmother, had been humble folk who didn't even know how to write their names. And if he were elected, Abe would be the first president born west of the Appalachian Mountains.

As the time approached for the delegation to arrive, Abe surveyed himself in the mirror. For a

moment he saw the man his wife constantly chided
him about. His hair was as unruly as ever, and he
had deep lines under his eyes. His clothes were
loose, his jacket hung off him like those on a
clothes rack, and his tie was permanently crooked.
Abe stared deep into the gray eyes in the mirror.
They looked weary at the mere thought of becoming president. During the campaign someone had
referred to him as "Old Abe," and the name had
stuck, even though Abe was eighteen years
younger than James Buchanan, the current president. And Abe had to admit, there was something
prematurely old about him.

Somewhere deep inside, Abe wondered whether
he really wanted the job of president at such a
troubled time as this. He knew that as the
Republican candidate he stood a good chance of
winning. This was because the more popular
Democratic party had split in two. Northern
Democrats met in Baltimore and nominated Abe's
old political foe Stephen Douglas as their candidate
for president. Southern Democrats, though, could
not bring themselves to think about electing a
Northerner. Instead they held their own convention in Richmond, Virginia, and nominated John
Breckinridge of Kentucky to be the Southern
Democratic candidate for president.

There was a knock at the door. Mary sailed into
the front room and glared at her husband. "Let
Willie get it," she said.

Abe nodded. He knew how much Mary hated
him answering the door. In her opinion it was a job
for servants and children.

Abe strolled up behind Willie at the open door and extended his huge hand to the man he recognized as the powerful Senator Ashmun of Massachusetts.

The senator smiled weakly, shook Abe's hand, and handed over a letter that officially informed Abe he had been chosen as the Republican candidate in the upcoming presidential election.

Soon the entire delegation of eight men was in the Lincolns' modest parlor. Abe had met only two of the men before; the rest he knew only by reputation. There were not enough chairs in the room for all the men to sit at once, so Willie and Tad were dispatched to bring in more chairs from the dining room, where Mary was laying out refreshments.

For once in his life, Abe was tongue-tied. Here in front of him was a group of men, most of whom he knew had supported his opponent William Seward. Indeed, several of the men seemed to be unable to keep scowls of disappointment off their faces. For a fleeting moment Abe wished he could excuse himself and walk out the back door to his law office, where he felt comfortable and secure. But, of course, he couldn't, so instead he tried to make polite conversation, all the while conscious of his thick Kentucky accent.

Slowly Abe began to relax. He cleared his throat and thanked the men for coming and promised to respond to their nomination in writing as soon as possible. He shook hands with each visitor and even managed a few jokes with them.

"How tall are you?" he asked William Kelley, the gangly delegate from Pennsylvania.

"Six foot three," William replied.

"I beat you!" Abe exclaimed. "I'm six foot four in my socks."

William Kelley laughed. "Pennsylvania bows to Illinois. I'm so glad we have found a candidate for the presidency whom we can look up to."

Mary walked into the room as the laughter was dying down and invited the men into the dining room. She poured glasses of water and cups of coffee for them to drink and offered teacakes and buns to eat. The men ate and drank heartily as Mary charmed them with her conversation.

The whole ordeal ended a lot more pleasantly than it had begun, and Abe hoped he had made a favorable impression with the men. After all, if he won, their lives were going to be entwined with his in the years ahead.

As was the custom, Abe did not campaign on his own behalf; he left that to other members of the Republican party. In fact, he did not leave Springfield between the time he was nominated in May and Election Day, six months later. But although he stayed in one place, he received plenty of visitors. Photographers came to take his picture. Reporters wanted details about his years growing up in Kentucky and Indiana. Others came to seek favors or to offer advice.

For every visitor who arrived on the doorstep, a hundred letters came in the mail. Some of the letters contained ugly threats to kill Abe and his family. A letter came from a man who had designed a "gold-plated, bulletproof" undershirt, which the man offered to produce for Abe.

One particular letter caught Abe's eye; it was from an eleven-year-old girl in Westfield, New York. Her name was Grace Bedell, and she wrote wishing Abe the best of luck in the upcoming election. In concluding her letter she gave him some advice, suggesting that he grow a beard. "You would look a great deal better, for your face is so thin.... All the ladies like whiskers, and they would tease their husbands to vote for you," she wrote. Grace also promised to convince her brothers to vote for the Republican party.

Abe gave the suggestion serious thought. He decided that Grace could well be right, and he started to grow a beard immediately. Whether his beard helped or not, no one could say, but on Election Day, November 6, 1860, Abraham Lincoln received 1,866,452 votes and carried every Northern state. Northern Democrat Stephen Douglas received 1,376,957 votes, and Southern Democrat Breckinridge 849,781. If the Democrats had stayed together, they would have easily beaten the Republicans. But they did not, and as a result, Abraham Lincoln was elected the sixteenth president of the United States.

As soon as the news arrived at the telegraph office in Springfield, the city erupted in celebration. Citizens sang in the street all night, fireworks lit the sky, and bands marched back and forth in front of the Lincolns' home. Mary joined Abe at Watson's Saloon, where the Republican women served a continuous supper for supporters. She wore a new dress she'd had made for the occasion.

It was two o'clock in the morning before Abe got to bed, but he could not sleep. Suddenly the reality of the situation settled on him. He was going to be the next president of the United States, and he had a dreadful feeling that some of the worst days for him personally, and for the country he loved so much, lay ahead.

It would be four months before President James Buchanan handed over the presidency, four months during which Abraham Lincoln would have the eyes of the nation on him but no power to bring about the healing he hoped would unite the country again.

As the months went by, Abe became increasingly worried about the mess he was inheriting. Time, instead of healing wounds, appeared to be opening up new ones. The Democrats were furious that they had lost the election, and Southern states began threatening to pull out of the Union altogether and form their own separate country. They even had a name for it, the Confederate States of America.

Everywhere Abe looked he saw signs of distrust and hatred. He had only to open his own mail to find sketches of him with a noose around his neck and chains around his feet, or a set of skull and crossbones drawn on a piece of paper announcing that someone was out to assassinate him. Abe tried not to take these threats personally.

As he waited to assume the presidency, Abe became more and more convinced that he needed to stand firm. No matter what happened, the Union had to be preserved. If they stayed together, Northern and Southern states could work out any problems they had with each other over slavery and states' rights. This became Abe's bottom line. He vowed he would never, under any circumstance, allow the South to separate from the North. The Founding Fathers had intended the country to stay together, and Abe would give his unswerving allegiance to following through on their intention.

Abe was not yet president when the situation began to go from bad to worse. A month after he was elected and three months before he was to take office, South Carolina announced it would no longer be a part of the United States of America. It was seceding from the Union to become its own sovereign nation.

In January Abe bid farewell to Mary as she went off to New York for two weeks to buy clothes befitting the wife of the new president. Although Abe was left to cook and clean for the two boys, he was glad that Mary had the opportunity to take her mind off the political problems gathering on the horizon. Every death threat they received made her more nervous.

Following South Carolina's lead, Florida, Mississippi, Alabama, Georgia, and Louisiana declared that they too were leaving the Union. Soon Texas was talking about seceding as well. Since there was little Abe could do about it until he became president, in early February 1861 he took a short trip east to Coles County to visit his stepmother. While he was there, he visited his father's grave and promised himself that as soon as he could find the time, he would make arrangements for a suitable tombstone to be laid on the grave.

It was difficult for Abe to say good-bye to the woman he had long considered his mother. As they stood together outside her log cabin, Abe told her how much he loved her.

"Don't be the president," she begged him, bursting into tears. "I fear something terrible will happen to you. I fear I will not see you again."

Abe put his arm around the seventy-three-year-old woman. "No. No, Mama. Trust in the Lord, and all will be well. We will see each other again."

February 10 was the Lincolns' last day in Springfield. Abe spent it visiting old friends. The last place he visited was his law office. He had handed the practice over to his partner, Billy Herndon, and they went over some of the legal cases at hand. When they were done, Abe lay down on the couch. His feet and legs dangled over the edge, as they always did. "You know, Billy," he said, "I'm sick of office-holding already, and I shudder to think of the tasks that are still ahead."

Billy nodded.

Abe continued. "How long have we been together?"

"More than sixteen years," came his partner's reply.

"We have never had a cross word during that time, have we?"

"No, we have not," Billy said.

They talked on for a while longer until Abe knew it was time to go. He still had to close up the trunks they were taking to Washington, D.C.

As he walked out the door, Abe looked back at the shingle hanging on the door. It read Lincoln & Herndon.

"Should I take it down?" Billy asked.

Abe shook his head. "Let it hang there undisturbed. It will give our clients the reassurance that the election of a new president brings no change in the firm of Lincoln and Herndon. If I live, I'm coming back sometime, and then we'll go right on practicing law as if nothing ever happened."

At seven-thirty in the morning, February 11, the day before Abe's fifty-second birthday, a thousand Springfield residents gathered at the Great Western Railroad depot to see Abraham Lincoln off to Washington.

Abe boarded the train, his hands firmly grasping the leather satchel that contained the only copy of his inaugural address. As he stood on the back platform of the train, he looked down through the drizzling rain into the eyes of people who had meant so much to him through the years. He had not intended to give a speech, but the words welled up within him. He lifted his hand, and the crowd grew silent.

"My friends," he began, his voice crackling with emotion, "no one, not in my situation, can appreciate my feeling of sadness at this parting. To this place, and the kindness of these people, I owe everything. Here I have lived a quarter of a century, and have passed from a young to an old man. Here my children have been born, and one is buried. I now leave, not knowing when, or whether ever, I may return, with a task before me greater than that which rested upon Washington. Without the assistance of that Divine Being, who ever attended him, I cannot succeed. With that assistance I cannot fail...let us confidently hope that all will yet be well. To His care commending you, as I hope in your prayers you will commend me, I bid you an affectionate farewell."

With that, the train whistle blew and Abe, accompanied by his family, began the long journey to Washington, D.C., and his place in history.

Chapter 16

The Sixteenth President of the United States

Abe was exhausted by the time he arrived in Washington, D.C., twelve days later. He was disturbed by the turn of events that had taken place in the South. At the train station in Albany, New York, he read the startling newspaper headline, "Jefferson Davis Sworn in as President of the Confederacy."

Then two days later in Philadelphia, Detective Pinkerton knocked on Abe's carriage door. His news was brief but stunning. Pinkerton told Abe he had uncovered an assassination plot when the train reached Baltimore. At first Abe was reluctant to believe the detective, but soon a telegram arrived from Washington with the same information. Abe knew the country would be thrown into chaos if he did not make it to his inauguration, so reluctantly he agreed to be transferred to another train.

Wearing a felt hat and a large overcoat as a disguise, he was secreted into Washington.

When his opponents heard about this not so grand entrance, they branded Abe a coward. Abe didn't mind too much. He expected to be the butt of all sorts of jokes and jibes. Mary, however, took the criticisms personally. She told Abe she planned to show these easterners just how sophisticated the Lincolns really were.

March 4, 1861, was a dismal, gray day. The sun tried to break through, but heavy clouds overpowered it. Rain threatened but did not fall. As Abe stood waiting for the carriage that would take him to his inauguration, he could not help but think that the weather mirrored his own feelings.

Soon Abe was seated next to President James Buchanan as the carriage bumped its way up Pennsylvania Avenue to the Capitol building. The journey was slow because an armed guard marched alongside the carriage. As Abe looked out the window, he could see thousands of people milling around. Many of the twenty-five thousand visitors to Washington for the inauguration had been unable to find anywhere to stay and had spent an uncomfortable night in shop doorways or public parks. The crowd was kept at bay by column after column of guards who lined the streets. Riflemen were positioned on the roofs of nearby buildings. Washington was as armed and ready for trouble as any fort during wartime.

Abe and President Buchanan were helped out of the carriage. Abe smoothed down his new black suit. The coachman handed him his gold-headed cane and silk stovepipe hat. Abe put on the hat and squared his shoulders. The two men walked through a temporary boarded tunnel that led to the inauguration platform. Abe knew the tunnel had been built to protect him from bullets, but he also knew that a gunman would have any number of opportunities to shoot him as he spoke, despite the fact that many plainclothes detectives mingled in the crowd.

The pair reached the platform, where three hundred dignitaries, including members of the Supreme Court, stood waiting. Abe nodded to the crowd in recognition and was guided to a chair in the front row. He looked around for somewhere to put his hat and cane but couldn't see a spot anywhere. Just then Stephen Douglas stepped forward and offered to hold them for Abe, who took his kind gesture as a good sign.

The ceremony soon got under way. Eighty-four-year-old Chief Justice Taney, who had sworn in the previous eight presidents, administered the oath of office. Soberly Abe put his hand on an open Bible and said, "I do solemnly swear that I will faithfully execute the office of President of the United States and will, to the best of my ability, preserve, protect, and defend the Constitution of the United States."

With these words, Abraham Lincoln became the sixteenth president of the United States. Guns boomed in an official salute, and a cheer rang out from the crowd.

When silence fell over the crowd again, Abe stepped forward to deliver his inaugural address. Deliberately, he took his reading glasses from his jacket pocket, unfolded his notes, and began to speak. "I have no purpose, directly or indirectly, to interfere with the institution of slavery in the States where it exists. I believe I have no lawful right to do so, and I have no inclination to do so.... No state, upon its own mere motion, can lawfully get out of the Union.... I shall take care, as the Constitution itself expressly enjoins upon me, that the laws of the Union shall be faithfully executed in all the States...."

Abe took a moment to look up. Ten thousand people were looking back at him, straining to catch every word he said. He finished his speech slowly and clearly so that every Southerner and every Southern sympathizer in the audience could understand the meaning of every word he said.

"In *your* hands, my dissatisfied fellow country-men, and not in *mine*, is the momentous issue of civil war. The government will not assail *you.* You can have no conflict without being yourselves the aggressors. *You* have no oath registered in Heaven to destroy the government, while *I* shall have the most solemn one to 'preserve, protect and defend' it.

"I am loath to close. We are not enemies, but friends. We must not be enemies. Though passion may have strained, it must not break our bonds of affection. The mystic chords of memory, stretching from every battlefield and patriot grave to every living heart and hearthstone all over this broad land, will yet swell the chorus of the Union when again touched, as surely they will be, by the better angels of our nature."

That night the Lincolns attended the inaugural ball along with Mary's sisters Ann and Elizabeth, who had come to enjoy the festivities. Abe was tired and ill at ease at the ball and spent most of the evening fiddling with his uncomfortably tight-fitting formal white gloves and thinking about how the American public would react to his speech. He hoped he had sounded firm but kind toward the Southern states.

Around nine the following morning, a carriage transported the Lincoln family from the Willard Hotel, where they had been staying, to the White House.

"Pa, can I have a goat?" pleaded eight-year-old Tad as they drove through the front gate. "You said once we got to Washington, I could have one."

"And you promised me a pony!" added ten-year-old Willie.

"Did I?" Abe asked, looking down at his two young sons. "Well, if that's what I said, then that's what you can have, though we'll have to get the iron fence mended in a few places first."

As the boys bounced up and down on the seat with excitement, Abe allowed himself a small smile. There had never been children in the White House before, and he was sure Tad and Willie would leave their mark.

At the White House Abe headed straight for his new office. Waiting for him on the desk was a report from Major Robert Anderson. Abe quickly glanced over the report and then sank into the leather chair behind the desk. The nightmare had begun.

The report said that provisions for the Union soldiers stationed at Fort Sumter were running low and would be exhausted in six weeks. A decision had to be made right away as to whether an attempt should be made to send more or the men should be allowed to surrender. Major Anderson estimated that about twenty thousand men would be needed to get the supplies safely through Confederate lines.

Abe considered the problem from all angles. Fort Sumter was a United States government fort located in the harbor mouth of Charleston, South Carolina. It was one of many pieces of land in the Southern states owned by the federal government. Of course, South Carolina, the first state to leave the Union, now claimed all such federal property within its boundary as its own. Abe could send men to Fort Sumter to reinforce the existing troops there, an act that would likely anger the South. Or he could do nothing and let the Confederacy take over federal property in the South. But this latter action would show the North to be weak and unprepared to fight for what belonged to it.

Neither solution appealed to Abe, and he had no advisers to turn to for help. The Senate had not yet confirmed any of the members of his cabinet or even authorized him to have a secretary.

Abe decided not to act until he had his cabinet in place and more information from General Scott, who was general in chief of the U.S. army. The days dragged on, and Abe became more anxious about what to do. One day he had such a bad headache he could not get out of bed. It was something that had never happened to him before.

The whole business of being president was depressing. The bottom floor of the White House was open to the public, and each time Abe descended the stairs from the living quarters he was besieged by people. For all but eight of the previous thirty years, Democrats had been in power. With being in power came the right to hand out thousands of jobs covering everything from postmasters and tax collectors to marshals and port managers. Now that a new administration was in power, it seemed to Abe that everywhere he turned he saw people carrying recommendations and demanding they be appointed to certain jobs.

In the midst of it all, Abe managed to pull together a cabinet. He also worked with Democrats who wanted the Union to be preserved. Stephen Douglas, his old political nemesis, promised to do all he could to raise troops and money for the cause.

Finally, on April 4, a month after the inauguration and with only two weeks of supplies left at Fort Sumter, Abe called for action. The Union would send an expeditionary fleet to Charleston. Its mission was not to create a war but to resupply the Union soldiers garrisoned at the fort. But in the eyes of the Confederacy, trying to resupply the fort amounted to an act of war.

No one in the White House was particularly surprised when news came that Confederate troops had opened fire on Fort Sumter in the predawn hours of April 12. The Union soldiers manning the fort held out for two days before they surrendered and were escorted to the dock to board a supply ship and sent back to the North.

As unpleasant as it was for Abe to admit, the cannon's bombarding Fort Sumter marked the first shots of the Civil War. Abe immediately issued a proclamation calling for seventy-five thousand men to volunteer to fight. These men would serve for ninety days, which Abe was sure would be long enough to get the South under control and back into the Union. Almost everyone agreed with this assumption. After all, the Union consisted of twenty-three states with a combined population of twenty-two million people. The Confederacy, on the other hand, consisted of only eleven states with nine million people, four million of whom were slaves. And it wasn't just that the North had more than twice the number of people, but most of the heavy industry was located there. Virtually all of the iron foundries, gun and ammunition factories, and shipyards were in the North. The North also had control of the navy and a better railway network.

Ninety days seemed plenty of time to defeat an enemy with so many seeming disadvantages. But there was one thing Abe and other Northerners did not take into account—the South had Jefferson Davis as its president. Davis was a brilliant and experienced army strategist. He had been trained at West Point, fought in the Mexican War, and served as President Pierce's Secretary of War. Few in the North were as shrewd in battle as Jefferson Davis was. Davis could take half the number of men and turn them into twice the fighting force.

The Confederate army was challenged when it heard of Abe's call for volunteers. Many Southerners talked of "fighting to the death" and making the South "a bloodbath where every man lay dead rather than surrender."

Jefferson Davis decided to move Confederate headquarters from Montgomery, Alabama, to Richmond, Virginia. Virginia had recently left the Union and joined the Confederacy along with Texas, Arkansas, Tennessee, and North Carolina.

While Abe had little time to think of anything else but the impending war, his wife had her own enemy to "attack." That enemy was the shoddy state of the White House. Mary explained to Abe that no one had looked after the White House properly for some time. Not one of the thirty-one rooms was fit for a president. The wallpaper was peeling, the ceilings were cracked, the drapes drooped, and the rugs were threadbare. At first Mary, who had been dubbed the "First Lady" by the *Times* of London newspaper, despaired over what to do about the state of the building. Then she discovered that every four years a sum of twenty thousand dollars was set aside for furnishings and decorations in the White House. Mary went straight to work planning her strategy. In mid-May 1861 she and several White House staff set out for New York, the government's pocketbook in hand.

Abe knew little of what Mary was up to and cared even less. Instead he was worried about the North. The first deaths of the Civil War were the result of fighting not between North and South but between Northerners fighting each other. On April 19, as the Sixth Massachusetts Infantry marched through Baltimore, Confederate sympathizers ambushed them, killing four soldiers.

These deaths, along with the unexpected death of Stephen Douglas from typhoid fever, bothered Abe a great deal. He began to wonder whether he really did have a solid army behind him. He was about to find out, as Union General Irwin McDowell had been ordered to march his troops into Virginia to take over the railroad junction at Manassas, about twenty-five miles southwest of Washington, D.C.

Mary returned from New York with rolls of flocked French wallpaper costing $6,800 and a $3,195 set of royal purple and gold china, each piece of which was emblazoned with the coat of arms of the United States. Abe did not inquire into how much it had all cost. He was too preoccupied with preserving the Union he had been elected to govern.

Sunday, July 21, 1861, was a warm, clear day in Washington, D.C. Early in the morning Abe and Mary made their way to the New York Avenue Presbyterian Church. Tad and Willie did not accompany their parents because it was too difficult to keep the children quiet during the service. As Abe looked out the carriage window, he saw hundreds of people headed west in buggies and gigs and on horseback. They looked as if they were on their way to a sporting event. The women wore pastel-colored summer dresses puffed up with crinolines and lace, and the men had on suits. Some had opera glasses slung around their necks, and many buggies were laden with amply stuffed picnic baskets. Newspaper reporters, notebooks tucked in their coat pockets, followed the throng.

Abe grimly surveyed the people. "You know, Mary, there are six senators going out to watch the proceedings."

"Are you sure we'll win?" Mary asked.

"We should," Abe replied. "General Scott complains our men are still green, but then, so are theirs."

"Where exactly are the armies going to meet?"

"If all goes according to plan, General McDowell should meet Confederate General Beauregard and his troops along a creek that runs into the Potomac. I'm told it's called Bull Run," Abe replied.

"I hope this battle finishes the secession problem once and for all so we can get back to being one country again," Mary said.

A cloud covered the sun as Abe helped Mary down from the carriage and escorted her into church.

Chapter 17

Dark Days

Abe and Mary Lincoln returned from church to the White House in time for a simple lunch. After he had eaten, Abe went over to General Scott's office to see how the battle between the North and South was progressing. He found Scott snoring on his couch. Abe shook him gently. When General Scott opened his eyes, Abe asked, "What news do you have?"

General Scott smiled as he held up a handful of telegrams. "Everything is going just as I predicted it would. I expect General McDowell to announce a Union victory at any time."

Abe sat down in the general's chair and read through the telegrams for himself. The messages described large Confederate losses, and Abe found himself agreeing with General Scott's assessment.

Relieved that the "war" was all but over, Abe went for a relaxing late Sunday afternoon buggy ride. He returned to the White House at six-thirty to find Secretary of State William Seward waiting for him inside the door, shaking and white as a ghost.

"The battle is lost," Seward said in barely a whisper. "The latest telegram says that McDowell is in full retreat through Centerville. The remnants of the Union army are scattered and will not re-form. Mr. President, we must take measures to save Washington."

As Abe heard the news, his heart dropped to his feet, though he tried not to show any sign of emotion right then. He had to think fast, or all could be lost. "Follow me," he said, handing his hat and coat to the doorman and setting off at a brisk pace for the War Department.

Other members of the cabinet began to gather as news of the defeat filtered out. Like most other residents of Washington, Abe worried that the Confederate army would take advantage of its victory and capture the largely unprotected city.

Later that evening, the first witnesses of the Battle of Bull Run came straggling back into the city. They were not the exuberant, expectant bunch Abe had seen leaving the capital early that morning. Many of the women were hysterical, and the men were grim-faced. Some were angry, others frightened.

Abe invited those he knew into the cabinet room and listened to their accounts of the battle. He learned that many of General McDowell's troops had fought with courage, but Confederate reinforcements had arrived, tipping the balance in the South's favor. In addition, some of the men who had signed up for the original ninety-day period were unwilling to risk their lives, since their time was up. At the sound of the first cannon, many of them had melted into the woods to watch the battle along with the spectators from Washington.

That night Abe got no sleep. The shock of losing the battle and the worry of what might happen next made sleep impossible. By dawn, it was raining. Abe stared out the White House windows at the troops returning to the city. The men were bloody, exhausted, and covered in mud. Some had lost everything, their knapsacks, caps, belts, even their boots, in the battle. As they poured up Pennsylvania Avenue, women ran out of houses and stores to offer them hot coffee. Some soldiers collapsed in doorways and were carried inside to be attended to.

The troops continued to straggle over the Long Bridge for the rest of the day as Abe met with his cabinet and tried to figure out what to do next. He realized it had been a mistake to lean so heavily on the advice of General Scott. Scott was a very experienced general, but at seventy-five, he appeared to be losing his fighting edge.

Abe and his cabinet decided that command of the eastern army should be given to General George McClellan, and the western troops to General John Fremont. They also agreed that the Union needed to tighten its naval blockade of the South to stop provisions and armaments from getting through to Confederate troops. Many more soldiers also needed to be called up, and for a lot longer than ninety days. As well, a plan was put forward to send Union troops into Virginia and Tennessee and up the Mississippi River at the same time.

At first Abe expected Washington to be attacked at any moment, but as the weeks dragged by, he realized that rather than mounting an attack, the Confederates were gathering up resources and training their troops.

As fall rolled around, the leaves on the trees in the White House grounds turned orange and then fluttered to the ground. Then the first snow of winter fell. Tad brought his goat inside to stay with him in his bedroom. Abe hardly noticed the astonishment of the staff at a goat being kept inside the White House.

Abe, along with the rest of the North, became more and more anxious about when the South would attack. Finally he decided that it was going to be up to Union troops to start the next engagement of the war and force the capitulation of the South. But every time Abe questioned General McClellan about when to launch such an attack, the answer was the same: The men needed more training. People began to grow impatient with this response. Even Congress joined in, pointing out that the war was supposed to have been over by now.

The Union army was now 500,000 strong, with many of the troops camped in tent cities along the Potomac River. One platoon was even encamped on the White House grounds. An army this size cost a lot of money to maintain, and some of those in charge took bribes to turn their eyes away from poor-quality deliveries. Abe was furious when he learned that government money had been spent on knapsacks held together by flour paste that dissolved in the first rain shower, boots that fell apart, blankets that were delivered moth-eaten, and pork so rotten not even hungry soldiers would touch it.

Deep down Abe suspected that many of his generals didn't know what they were doing, so he decided to learn as much as he could about military strategy. He turned to books, just as he had when he had learned how to become a surveyor and a lawyer. He would often study long into the night and be awakened early in the morning with the two boys climbing over him, begging for a wrestling match. Their antics always made Abe smile. Indeed, it was about the only thing that managed to make him smile during the long, dark days of the Civil War. By now, Tad had a small cart that was pulled by a pony. He was often spotted trying to coax the pony and cart through the bottom floor of the White House. However, he could not seem to train the pony to climb the stairs.

The boys discovered that all of the bell chords for summoning servants to various rooms came together in the attic, and they often sneaked up there to yank all the cords at once. This sent maids and footmen scurrying in all directions. Mary had the state dining room set up as a schoolroom, but none of the tutors she hired stayed long. They accused the boys of being wild, though Abe and Mary insisted they were simply high spirited.

Not everyone found fault with the boys. Some of the Union soldiers camped on the White House lawn welcomed the laughs the Lincoln boys gave them. No one could resist smiling when the boys used sheets and ropes to rig the flat roof of the White House to resemble the deck of a ship. The boys spent hours taking turns spotting enemy ships through an old telescope one of the generals had given to Willie.

Even Secretary of War Edwin Stanton, a man not noted for his love of children, grew to love the boys. He commissioned Tad as one of his lieutenants and had a small uniform made for him. When Tad received it, he decided to see how much "power" it really gave him. He called the doormen, cooks, gardeners, and stable hands together. He then dismissed the regular soldiers who guarded the White House and ordered the household staff to take their places on guard duty. They all obeyed young Lieutenant Lincoln. When Abe heard about this, he roared with laughter and then waited until Tad had worn himself out and fallen asleep before he carried him up to bed and dismissed the confused household staff.

Opportunities to laugh became rare as the war dragged on. Mary tried her best to continue a "normal" life as the First Lady. In January 1862 she was preparing for the largest party the Lincolns had hosted in the White House. Any kind of party at the White House was rare because the president had no entertainment budget. All of the food and drink consumed at the White House was paid from the president's own salary. Mary did all she could to make the party a lavish affair for the five hundred distinguished guests she had hand selected. The serving staff was outfitted in new purple uniforms to match the expensive china she had purchased. Mary also hired Maillard's of New York, the country's finest caterer, to provide the food for the event, since, as she told Abe, there wasn't a single caterer in Washington fit to work for the White House.

By the night of the party, the Lincolns' attention was focused elsewhere. Willie lay sick in bed. The doctors couldn't be sure what his illness was, though they told Abe it was probably typhoid. The word sent shivers down Abe's spine. The illness had no cure.

At the party, Abe's ears were listening to the United States Marine Band play, but his heart was upstairs with his son. Mary, who tried not to cry in public, wore a forced smile as she mingled with the guests. Between songs the two worried parents took turns slipping out to see how their son was doing. Willie had a high temperature and was in and out of consciousness.

Abe and Mary managed to survive the evening, though Mary scarcely noticed when the party was reported as "the most superb affair of its kind ever seen here."

During the next few days, Willie became weaker, and then Tad came down with the same illness. But while Tad began to slowly recover, eleven-year-old

Willie did not. On February 20, 1862, Abe stood at the foot of his son's bed and watched Willie draw his last breath. Abe stood there a long time before going downstairs to tell his family. Finding his private secretary first, he blurted out, "Well, Nicolay, my boy is gone—he is actually gone!" He burst into deep sobs and walked away quickly to find Tad and Mary.

Later that night, Abe lay down beside Tad, and they wept together. Abe mourned the loss of a second son to disease, and Tad the loss of a brother who had been his constant companion. Abe did not have as much success consoling his wife. Mary became hysterical when she heard the news and refused to be comforted.

William Lincoln's funeral was held in the Green Room of the White House, where the boy's impishness had won him many friends. Mary did not attend the service; she would not get out of bed. After the funeral Abe locked himself in his office and wept bitterly. Death seemed to be all around him. Every day other men's sons, many not much older than Willie, were being slaughtered on the battlefield. In a two-day battle near Shiloh Church in Tennessee, thirteen thousand Union soldiers were killed or seriously wounded. And that was just one battle. With all his heart, Abe wished the war could be over.

Besides coping with his own grief, Abe became increasingly worried about his wife. Mary had become what the newspapers called "unbalanced." She wept and moaned in her bed for three months, not even getting up to nurse Tad back to full strength from his bout with sickness. Abe had to employ a nurse to stay with her for fear she might harm herself. Finally Mary ordered some black clothes for mourning and managed to leave her room. However, she could never face going into the Green Room or Willie's bedroom again. She even had the Marine Band stop its concerts on the White House lawn because the music reminded her of the last days with Willie.

Abe began to take a more active role in the war, and when he did, the North began to gain some victories. In spring 1862 Union troops moved up the Mississippi River, eventually taking control of New Orleans before becoming bogged down at Vicksburg, Mississippi. But by June the tide was turning again. Against Abe's advice, General McClellan insisted on landing troops on the Yorktown Peninsula in Virginia and marching his men seventy-five miles overland to launch a "surprise" rear attack on Richmond, the Confederate capital. His troops, however, made such slow progress up the peninsula that the South had ample warning of an impending attack. The Union army made it to the outskirts of Richmond, where the soldiers rested and were surprised when Confederate troops under the command of General Robert E. Lee attacked them. Seven days of bloody fighting occurred before Union forces were driven back to the James River. When the roll was called, twenty-three thousand Union soldiers were dead, wounded, or unaccounted for.

With the defeat, public confidence in General McClellan fell to an all-time low, and Abe replaced him as general in chief of the army with General Henry Halleck, who was nicknamed "Old Brains." Abe soon found out the nickname suited him well. General Halleck could plan things out in his head, but he lacked the courage to order men into battle.

While battles were being won and lost, the cause of ending slavery continued to gain strength. Abolitionists wanted Abe to punish the Confederate South by declaring all slavery illegal so that once the South was conquered, there would be no more slavery.

Abe was reluctant to make such a declaration and kept telling people, "We didn't go to war to put down slavery, but to put the flag back." Besides, there were many Northerners—especially those living in Kentucky, Delaware, Maryland, and Missouri, the four slave-holding states that had remained loyal to the Union—who supported the idea of popular sovereignty that Stephen Douglas had put forward. Still, abolitionists kept pushing Abe to declare slavery illegal everywhere in the United States, even on Confederate land.

Abe replied that he did not have the power to set slaves free. No president did. However, the slave problem was never far from his thoughts. He knew that without their four million black slaves, the Confederate states would face a grave shortage of labor and be severely weakened. Such a situation would bring the war to a much faster close. Abe wondered, too, what would happen if the South surrendered and slavery was allowed to continue there? Nothing would have been resolved, and the stage could well be set for another Civil War in the future. Above all else, Abe wanted to avoid this. He vowed to do all in his power to make this the last time in the country's history that the blood of one brother would be shed at the hands of another.

Abe realized that he *did* have a power he had not yet used. As commander in chief of the Armed Forces, during wartime, the president had the power to make executive decrees. This meant that if he thought something would so weaken the enemy as to hasten the end of hostilities, he could, in the best interests of the country, make it law without going through the usual channels. This gave Abe a means through which to address the issue of slavery.

Once he had made up his mind to use a decree to end slavery, Abe worked on a secret plan to make it happen. He dared not tell anyone for fear of the uproar such an announcement could cause.

On September 22, 1862, Abe held the final draft of his "Emancipation Proclamation." The document stated that if the South did not return to the Union by January 1, 1863, as President of the United States, Abe would declare all slaves in Confederate states free for all time. This decree did not include the slaves in the four slave-owning Union states. Abe had a separate, more gradual plan to end slavery there.

By the following morning, the Emancipation Proclamation had been printed in every newspaper in the United States, and the waiting began. Would the South surrender before the deadline or not?

On New Year's Day, 1863, the South was silent. Abe had his answer. He gathered his cabinet together, and the men watched him sign the document that forever freed millions of Americans. Instead of signing the proclamation A. Lincoln, as he usually did, Abe signed his full name. As he put the pen down, he turned to the men serving in his cabinet and said, "If my name ever goes into history, it will be for this act."

Within a short time, the Union formed all-black regiments made up mainly of the 180,000 ex-slaves who had escaped from the South. Such regiments upset many white people, since it meant that blacks would be allowed to shoot whites in battle. Many Northerners found it hard to adjust to the whole idea of emancipation and black soldiers. They began to put pressure on Abe to stop the draft, sign a truce with the South, and take back the proclamation of emancipation. Abe would not budge. He told people, "I am a slow walker, but I never walk backwards." He would not give up until the war was won and every slave in the Confederacy was free.

Those who actively agitated for a truce with the South were called "copperheads," after the poisonous snake. Abe knew he had to make sure they did not get their way. He gave authorization for any copperhead to be arrested if he talked of rebellion against the government. By summer 1863, thirteen thousand copperheads were in jail. Those who escaped jail organized riots, set fires, and killed

black men and women, along with any white people who tried to save them.

It seemed to Abe that now as many Northerners
as Southerners hated him. Still, he pressed on.

Abe could not find a general who was as good
as the South's General Robert E. Lee. General
McClellan dug his troops in at Antietam when he
should have pushed forward and routed the enemy.
Wearily Abe dismissed McClellan from command
and replaced him with General Burnside. Almost
immediately, General Burnside's bungling led to
the loss of twelve thousand Union soldiers at
Fredericksburg, Virginia. Burnside had to go, and
General Hooker took his place. Hooker was vain
and pompous, which Abe could stand if he won
battles. Alas, he did not. His troops were defeated
at Chancellorsville, where seventeen thousand
Union soldiers lost their lives.

General Meade replaced General Hooker, and
he led his troops into the small town of Gettysburg,
Pennsylvania. There, Union and Confederate troops
fought a fierce battle that lasted three days, ending
on July 4, 1863. One hundred seventy thousand
soldiers were involved in the fighting, and when
the battle was over, fifty thousand of them lay dead
or severely wounded. Union forces won the battle,
and as Robert E. Lee led his decimated Confederate
army in retreat, Abe wired General Meade with the
order, "Do not let the enemy escape." He knew that
capturing and destroying Lee's ravaged army was
key to ending the war. General Meade, however,
decided that his men were tired and needed time to

rest and recover, so he disobeyed the order. While Union troops rested, the Confederate army, which was just as exhausted, fled back across the Potomac and out of the grasp of General Meade.

When Abe heard what the general had done, he was furious. This had been the Union's best chance for some decisive action, and General Meade had hesitated. Abe began to wonder just how long the war could go on. Would it continue until there were no more men left who were fit to fight?

Not only did the government have to pay for wages, supplies, and clothing for its soldiers, but also it had to dig graves for those killed in action. In this regard, a national cemetery was established at Gettysburg to hold the bodies of the soldiers who lost their lives in the battle there. Four months later Abe was asked to make a few remarks at the dedication of the cemetery, where Edward Everett, a noted orator from Massachusetts, would be the main speaker.

Abe wrote out his address on a single sheet of paper. When he was done, he counted the words. There were two hundred sixty-nine of them. He had been asked for a few remarks, and that is what he would give the gathered crowd.

On a brisk autumn morning, November 19, 1863, Abe stood on the speaker's platform looking out over the Gettysburg battlefield where so many brave men from both sides had died in battle. Unfolding the sheet of paper, he began his address.

Four score and seven years ago our fathers brought forth on this continent a new nation, conceived in Liberty and dedicated to the proposition that all men are created equal.

Now we are engaged in a great civil war, testing whether that nation or any nation so conceived and so dedicated can long endure. We are met on a great battle-field of that war. We have come to dedicate a portion of it as a final resting place for those who here gave their lives that that nation might live. It is altogether fitting and proper that we should do this.

But, in a larger sense, we can not dedicate—we can not consecrate—we can not hallow this ground. The brave men, living and dead, who struggled here have consecrated it, far above our poor power to add or detract. The world will little note, nor long remember what we say here, but it can never forget what they did here. It is for us the living, rather, to be dedicated here to the unfinished work which they who fought here have thus far so nobly advanced. It is rather for us to be here dedicated to the great task remaining before us—that from these honored dead we take increased devotion to that cause for which they gave the last full measure of devotion—that we here highly resolve that these dead shall not have died in vain—that this nation, under God, shall have a new birth of freedom—and that government of the people, by the people, for the people, shall not perish from the Earth.

When Abe was finished, the crowd clapped politely, though no one was particularly impressed by his speech. However, the Battle of Gettysburg did boost the morale of Union soldiers, who began winning more battles. As they did so, Abe started hearing good reports about General Ulysses S. Grant, who had won the siege at Vicksburg. In the winter of 1864, Abe summoned the general to Washington, where he appointed him the new general in chief of the Union forces.

Finally, Abraham Lincoln knew he had a man who was up to the job. General Grant soon gained the title "Unconditional Surrender Grant." In battle after battle, the South was beaten back, though not without heavy Union casualties. By summer, fifty-four thousand more Union soldiers had been either killed or severely wounded in the fighting. The high number of casualties saddened Abe, but he still believed that General Grant was making the best tactical decisions for the army.

The country, though, was not so sure. Another presidential election was looming, and there was a growing movement to use it to oust Abraham Lincoln and end the war without further bloodshed. George McClellan, the former general whom Abe had dismissed from command, ran as the Democratic candidate. He proposed peace with the South at any price.

This time Abe's vice-presidential running mate was Andrew Johnson. Public opinion, however, was running so high against Abe because of the war that there seemed little likelihood that they would win the election. Indeed, Abe began writing notes to himself about the best way to hand over power to the Democrats.

As the election approached, something unexpected happened. Union General William Tecumseh Sherman marched his army from Tennessee into Georgia and after a short siege captured the city of Atlanta. About the same time, General Philip Sheridan was winning the battle against Confederate forces in the Shenandoah Valley, and General Grant was closing in on Richmond, the Confederate capital.

Finally the end of the Civil War was in sight, and with victory close at hand, the voters began to see Abe differently. They no longer saw him as a man who was willing to inflict indefinite suffering on the American people. Instead he was the man who had guided the Union in defeat of the South. The eventual reunification of the country was imminent. And now that the war was winding down, surely Abe deserved a chance to heal the wounds of the country.

On Election Day, November 8, 1864, Abraham Lincoln won the election by a landslide of over four million votes. To Abe's surprise, he was going to serve a second term as president.

Chapter 18

A Single Shot

As the war began to wind down, Abe began to worry about the language he was hearing in Congress and in the North generally. There was talk of "paying the South back" and "making them regret that they had ever killed a Union soldier." This kind of attitude made Abe nervous. All along he had been fighting to reunite the North and South. The last thing he wanted was for bitterness and anger to enter the process, possibly setting the stage for another war.

In his second inaugural address on March 4, 1865, Abe tried to make people understand that the country was like two brothers who'd had a squabble. Now it was time to forgive each other and go forward. He said:

Fondly do we hope—fervently do we pray—that this mighty scourge of war may speedily pass away.... With malice toward none, with charity for all, with firmness in the right, as God gives us to see the right, let us strive on to finish the work we are in, to bind up the nation's wounds, to care for him who shall have borne the battle, and for his widow and his orphan—to do all which may achieve and cherish a just and lasting peace among ourselves and with all nations.

Abe had no idea as he spoke these words that his wife was about to become one of the last women widowed by the Civil War and his children the orphans he so eloquently asked the American people to care for.

The crowd cheered and waved flags when the speech was over, and the new vice president Andrew Johnson swaggered to his feet. He had taken too much alcohol to calm his nerves before the inauguration and was now quite drunk.

At his first inauguration Abe had inherited a country on the verge of war; now it was on the verge of peace. But the price of peace had been higher than anyone had imagined. Even as the inauguration was taking place, General Sherman and his Union troops were marching from North Carolina to meet up with General Grant's army. As he went, Sherman was laying waste to everything in his path as a way of showing people in the South that rebellion comes with a price.

A month later, on April 2, Abe received the news that Confederate President Jefferson Davis and his government were fleeing from Richmond, torching warehouses and bridges as they went. When dawn broke the following morning, Union troops marched into Richmond and hoisted the United States flag, which had not flown over the state in four years.

Abe was very curious to visit the site of the "other presidency," and so two days after Jefferson Davis abandoned Richmond, he and Tad sailed up the James River, accompanied by a small military guard.

As Richmond came into view, Abe sat in stunned silence. Smoke still hung over the city. Through the haze he could see the smashed facades of buildings and rubble-strewn streets. There was barely a white face to be seen. Freed slaves and black Union troops scurried about trying to put out the fires that still burned.

As Abe stepped ashore, a black man putting out a fire with shovelfuls of dirt recognized him. "Bless the Lord, there is the great Messiah!" he yelled, throwing his shovel aside and falling to his knees. Others joined in with shouts of "Praise the Lord, Father Abraham come," and "Glory Hallelujah!" as the man tried to kiss Abe's boots.

"Don't kneel to me," Abe said quickly, helping the man to his feet. "That's not right. You must kneel to God only, and thank Him for the liberty you will hereafter enjoy."

Once inside the now abandoned Confederate president's residence, Abe walked into Jefferson

Davis's office. He stood beside the desk and sat in Davis's chair. The soldiers who accompanied him cheered loudly as he did so. Abe picked up a handful of one-thousand-dollar Confederate bonds from the floor. At the height of the war these had been worth the amount of money printed on them. Now they were worthless. He dropped them, and as they fluttered to the floor, he thought of all the money, buildings, and especially people that had been wasted by the terrible war. Three million men, many of them just teenagers, had fought, and six hundred thousand of them had been killed. Among the dead were three of Mary Lincoln's half-brothers and two of her brothers-in-law, who had fought on the side of the Confederacy.

The war was now in its final throes, and Abe looked forward to the day when he could officially declare it over and begin the process of healing the people and the land they had fought so bitterly upon.

Jefferson Davis was a stubborn man; he refused to accept the inevitability of defeat and ordered his troops to fight on in the countryside. Finally, on April 9, 1865, General Robert E. Lee could see no point in fighting on. He and General Grant met at the Appomattox Courthouse in Virginia, where he surrendered his forces. The Civil War was over.

When Abe received the telegram informing him of Robert E. Lee's surrender, he was overjoyed. He rushed to tell Mary and Tad the wonderful news. Soon the whole of Washington was celebrating as never before. Cannons boomed loudly, bands struck up tunes, and people flocked into the streets.

With the war over, Abe was busier than ever. Many members of the government wanted to punish the South, but he was convinced they should invest time and money to rebuild it; thus, the era known as Reconstruction began.

Although Abe was working eighteen-hour days, he felt better than he had in years. He had a spring in his step and a smile on his face as he went about the business of being the leader of a country finally at peace.

On Good Friday, April 14, Abe found time to go for a buggy ride with Mary. Just as he was getting ready to leave his office and collect Mary, he heard a commotion outside his office door. He opened the door to see a black woman being escorted away by two guards.

"But I need to see Mr. Lincoln!" the woman pleaded.

"I'm here. Tell me what you want. I have time for all who need me. Let the good woman come in," Abe said.

The guards let the woman go.

Alone in Abe's office, the woman let her words come tumbling out in a jumble. Her name was Nancy Bushrod, and she had been a slave at the old Harwood Plantation near Richmond. When the Emancipation Proclamation had been issued, Nancy, her husband, Tom, and their three children had fled to Washington. Tom had joined the army. At first his pay had arrived every month, but now it had stopped coming. Nancy and her children were starving. She wanted the president to help her find out what had happened to her husband's paychecks.

Abe looked at Nancy Bushrod for a long moment. She was like so many millions of other Americans, black and white, whose lives had been turned upside down by the war. All of them would need help and direction to get back on their feet again.

Finally Abe spoke gently. "You are entitled to your soldier-husband's pay. Come this time tomorrow and the papers will be signed and ready for you to collect his wages."

Nancy burst into tears; she tried to speak but could not.

Abe looked her in the eye. "My good woman, perhaps you'll see many a day when all the food in the house is a single loaf of bread. Even so, give every child a slice and send your children to school." He then bowed and opened the door for her.

Nancy Bushrod left the room, and Abe could hear her sobbing all the way to the front door. He made some notes on her case on a sheet of paper and reached for his hat. It was time to take a ride with Mary.

As they rode down Pennsylvania Avenue, Abe waved and smiled at everyone.

"Dear husband, you almost startle me with your great cheerfulness," Mary said, reaching out to hold his hand.

Abe thought about what she said. It *was* true. He was really happy for the first time in four years. The burden of war had been removed from him. He replied, "And well I may feel so, Mary. I consider this day, the war has come to a close. We must both be more cheerful in the future—between the war and the loss of our darling Willie—we have both been very miserable."

He watched as Mary smiled in agreement.

When he got back to the White House, Abe had a meeting at the War Department. He arrived a few minutes ahead of the others and found himself talking to Bill Crook, one of his White House guards. "Crook," Abe said, "do you know I believe there are men who want to take my life?" He paused for a moment and then muttered, "And I have no doubt they will do it."

Bill Crook looked surprised. "Why do you think so, Mr. President?"

"Other men have been assassinated," Abe replied.

"I hope you are mistaken, Mr. President."

Abe stood deep in thought for a moment, and then he said, "I have perfect confidence in those who are around me—in every one of you men. I know no one could do it and escape alive. But if it is to be done, it is impossible to prevent it."

Later that night Abe and Mary were scheduled to see a play called *Our American Cousin* at the nearby Ford's Theatre. They were to be accompanied by two friends, Major Rathbone and Miss Clara Harris.

The group was late arriving, and as they settled into the flag-draped presidential box, the play stopped and the orchestra struck up the tune "Hail to the Chief," which Abe loved to hear played. A cheer went up from the approximately seventeen hundred members of the audience as they rose to their feet.

Abe stepped forward, smiled, bowed to the crowd, and then settled into a rocking chair that had been specially placed in the box for him, Mary close by his side.

The play was one that Abe had not seen before. It was a comedy about an American man who goes to England to claim an inheritance and ends up in the hands of a scheming woman. A particularly funny line of dialogue was delivered by one of the actors, and the audience erupted into loud laughter. Abe laughed as well. As they laughed, no one noticed the door to the presidential box open and then shut.

Bang! A single shot rang out from a small derringer, the sound barely audible over the laughter of the crowd.

Abe slumped forward, blood running from behind his left ear.

Mary Lincoln let out an ear-piercing scream.

The gunshot had been fired at exactly 10:13 P.M., April 14, 1865.

President Abraham Lincoln did not die immediately. Unconscious and bleeding, he was carried to a nearby house belonging to the Petersen family. None of the beds were long enough for him, so he was laid diagonally across a bed. Two doctors who had been in the audience at Ford's Theatre watched over the president, though they acknowledged there was little they could do. Three more doctors, including the Lincoln family doctor and the Surgeon General, arrived and came to the same conclusion. It was only a matter of time before the president's body gave up the fight.

People came and went from the room. Mary became so hysterical she had to be escorted out, only to beg to be allowed to return to the side of her dying husband. Robert Lincoln was summoned and stood miserably at his father's side. Members of Congress pressed around the bed, too, unable or unwilling to admit what they were seeing.

Heavy rain fell as the night wore on, and just after dawn on April 15, fifty-six-year-old Abraham Lincoln drew his last breath. A doctor closed his eyes and pulled the sheet over his head. Edwin Stanton, Secretary of War, bowed his head and said, "Now he belongs to the ages."

Within minutes every bell in Washington, D.C., began to toll as stunned crowds gathered to weep and mourn in the streets.

Chapter 19

A Nation Mourns

It did not take long to piece together the assassination plot. John Wilkes Booth, a well-known actor, had taken it upon himself to make one last attempt to win the war. His plan involved two other men, George Atzerodt and Lewis Paine. George Atzerodt was to kill Vice President Andrew Johnson, Lewis Paine was to kill Secretary of State William Seward, and John Wilkes Booth himself would put a bullet in President Lincoln's head. To add to the dramatic effect, Booth decreed that all three murders should take place at exactly 10:15 P.M. (though Booth ended up firing his fatal shot two minutes early). Once they had accomplished their deed, the plan called for the men to escape to the South, where they believed they would be heralded as heroes by Confederate sympathizers.

Booth thought that killing these three key leaders would throw the government into such turmoil that it would give the South an opportunity to rally again.

Only one of the three assassinations went as planned. George Atzerodt decided he could not murder anyone. He pawned his revolver for ten dollars and started on foot for his home twenty miles outside the city. Lewis Paine entered William Seward's house with a gun and a knife. He found the Secretary of State lying in bed, but when he pulled the trigger, his gun misfired. Instead Lewis beat William Seward over the head with the pistol. Other members of the household heard Seward's cries for help and came rushing to assist him. Knife in hand, Lewis Paine dashed down the stairs and out the door. He left behind five gashed and bleeding people, all of whom recovered from their injuries. Only John Wilkes Booth was successful, shooting the unsuspecting president in the left side of the head, creating a wound from which he died early the next morning.

And what about President Lincoln's personal bodyguard? John Parker had wanted to see the play himself. Instead of staying at his post outside the door to the presidential box, he had slipped downstairs to find a seat and watch the show.

After John Wilkes Booth shot the president, he leaped fifteen feet down from the theatre box onto the stage. On the way down, one of his spurs caught on a flag draping the presidential box, causing him to fall and breaking a bone in his lower leg in the process. Scrambling to his feet, he yelled, "Sic semper tyrannis" ("Thus always to tyrants"), the state motto of Virginia. He limped across the stage and escaped out the back door of the theatre, where he had a horse waiting.

The conspiracy was uncovered the next morning when Booth's sister came forward with a letter he had left in her care that spelled out his intention to kill the president. A massive manhunt was begun, and twelve days later on April 26, 1865, John Wilkes Booth was cornered in a tobacco barn in Virginia. Soldiers and detectives surrounded the barn, and Booth was shot and killed.

President Lincoln's body lay in an open casket in the East Room of the White House. After the funeral service on April 19, the casket was taken up Pennsylvania Avenue to the Capitol, escorted by a regiment of black soldiers. At the Capitol thousands of people lined up for one last glimpse of the president who had led them to peace.

Mary Lincoln wanted her husband to be buried in Springfield, Illinois, where they had spent their happiest years together. On April 21 a funeral train set out from Washington, D.C. It retraced the route Abe had traveled when he came to Washington to assume the presidency.

The United States mourned as it had never mourned before. On the eve of peace, the man with the unswerving commitment to rebuild a strong and united country had been taken away. The railway was lined with soldiers and civilians, blacks and whites, all standing silently, paying their last respects. At every stop funeral services were held, and columns of numb citizens filed past the open casket for one last look at the fallen president.

As the train puffed across the Illinois prairie, bonfires lined the tracks as simple farmers tried to express their grief for the man who had once lived among them.

Abraham Lincoln's body lay in state in Springfield. Tens of thousands of people came to pay their last respects. Then, finally, one last funeral service was held, and the body was buried at Oak Ridge Cemetery.

As might be expected, Mary Lincoln did not deal well with the death of her husband. And her grief was added to in July 1871, when Tad Lincoln died at eighteen years of age from an infection in his lungs.

Mary was unable to settle down anywhere for long after her husband's assassination, and she died on July 15, 1882, from a stroke.

Like his father, Robert Todd Lincoln became a lawyer in Illinois, where he married and had three children.

Today, over a million people each year visit Abraham Lincoln's grave in Springfield, Illinois. And there is one question that many of these people have on their minds: *How would the United States be different if Abraham Lincoln had not been assassinated?* It is the great unanswerable question.

Baker, Jean H., *Mary Todd Lincoln: A Biography*, W. W. Norton, 1987.

Donald, David Herbert, *Lincoln*, Simon & Schuster, 1995.

Freedman, Russell, *Lincoln: A Photobiography*, Clarion Books, 1987.

Sandburg, Carl, *Abraham Lincoln: The Prairie Years and the War Years* (one-volume edition), Harcourt, 1974.

Thomas, Benjamin P., *Abraham Lincoln: A Biography*, Alfred A. Knopf, 1952.

Warren, Louis A., *Lincoln's Youth: Indiana Years 1816–1830*, Indiana Historical Society, 1959.

Janet and Geoff Benge are a husband and wife writing team with more than twenty years of writing experience. Janet is a former elementary school teacher. Geoff holds a degree in history. Together they have a passion to make history come alive for a new generation of readers.

Originally from New Zealand, the Benges make their home in the Orlando, Florida, area.

Also from Janet and Geoff Benge...